Allyn & Bacon Casebook Series
Mental Health

Edited by

Jerry L. Johnson

Grand Valley State University

George Grant, Jr.

Grand Valley State University

PEARSON

Boston   New York   San Francisco
Mexico City   Montreal   Toronto   London   Madrid   Munich   Paris
Hong Kong   Singapore   Tokyo   Cape Town   Sydney

To all of those who have helped, advised, supported, criticized,
and forgiven. You know who you are.
Jerry L. Johnson

To my wife, Beverly, who inspires and supports me
in all my endeavors. In loving memory of my father and mother,
George and Dorothy Grant.
George Grant, Jr.

Series Editor: *Patricia Quinlin*
Marketing Manager: *Kris Ellis-Levy*
Production Administrator: *Janet Domingo*
Compositor: *Galley Graphics*
Composition Buyer: *Linda Cox*
Manufacturing Buyer: *JoAnne Sweeney*
Cover Coordinator: *Rebecca Krzyzaniak*

For related titles and support materials, visit our online catalog at www.ablongman.com.

Copyright © 2005 Pearson Education, Inc.

Library of Congress Cataloging-in-Publication Data

Allyn & Bacon casebook series for mental health / edited by Jerry L. Johnson, George
  Grant, Jr.—1st ed.
    p. cm.
  Includes bibliographical references.
  ISBN 0-205-38947-3 (pbk.)
    1. Psychiatric social work—Case studies.   2. Social case work.   I. Title: Allyn and Bacon
  casebook series for mental health.   II. Title: Casebook series for mental health.   III. Johnson,
  Jerry L.   IV. Grant, George, Jr.
  HV689. A52 2005
  362.2′0425—dc22

                                                                              2004056835

Printed in the United States of America

10 9 8 7 6 5 4 3 2 1   09 08 07 06 05 04

Contents

Preface

This text offers students the chance to study the work of experienced social workers practicing in mental health practice settings. As graduate and undergraduate social work educators, we (the editors) have struggled to find quality practice materials that translate well into a classroom setting. Over the years, we have used case materials from our practice careers, professionally produced audio-visuals, and tried other casebooks. While each had its advantages, we could not find a vehicle that allowed students to study the work of experienced practitioners that took students beyond the belief that practice is a technical endeavor that involves finding "correct" interventions to solve client problems.

We want our students to study and analyze how experienced practitioners think about practice and how they struggle to resolve ethical dilemmas and make treatment decisions that meet the needs of their clientele. We want students to review and challenge the work of others in a way that allows them to understand what comprises important practice decisions with real clients in real practice settings. That is, we want classroom materials that allow students entry into the minds of experienced practitioners.

Goals of the Casebook

This Casebook focuses on practice with clients dealing with mental health in a variety of settings and from diverse backgrounds. Our goal is to provide students with an experience that:

1. Provides personal and intimate glimpses into the thinking and actions of experienced practitioners as they work with clients. In each case, students may demonstrate their understanding of the cases and how and/or why the authors approached their case in the manner presented.

2. Provides a vehicle to evaluate the process, ideas, and methods used by the authors. We also wanted to provide students a chance to present their ideas about how they would have worked differently with the same case.
3. Affords students the opportunity to use evidence-based practice findings (Gibbs, 2003; Cournoyer, 2004) as part of the case review and planning process. We challenge students to base practice judgments and case planning exercises on current practice evidence available through library and/or electronic searches, and practice wisdom gained through consultation and personal experience when the evidence is conflicted or lacking.

To meet our goals, the cases we included in this text focus on the practice process, specifically client engagement, assessment, and the resultant clinical process, including the inevitable ethical dilemmas that consistently arise in daily practice. We aim to demonstrate the technical and artistic elements involved in developing and managing the various simultaneous processes involved in practice. While we recognize the difficulty of presenting process information (circular) in a linear medium (book), we have tried to do the best job possible toward this end.

To achieve our goals, we include four in-depth case studies in this text. In the case studies, authors guide students through the complete practice process, from initial contact to client termination and practice evaluation. Focusing heavily on multi-systemic client life history (see Chapter 1), students get a detailed look into the life history and presentation of the client. Then, we challenge students by using client information and classroom learning to develop a written narrative assessment, diagnostic statement, treatment and intervention plan, termination and follow-up plan, and a plan to evaluate practice. We have used these cases as in-class exercises, the basis for semester-long term papers, and as comprehensive final examinations that integrate multifaceted student learning in practice courses across the curriculum.

Rationale

As former practitioners, we chose the cases carefully. Therefore, the cases in this text focus on the process (thinking, planning, and decision-making) of social work practice and not necessarily on techniques or outcome. Do not be fooled by this statement. Obviously, we believe in successful client outcome based, at least in part, on the use of evidence-based practice methods and current research findings. As important as this is, it is not our focus here—with good reason. Our experience suggests that instructive process occurs in cases that have successful and unsuccessful outcome. In fact, we often learned more from unsuccessful cases than successful cases. We learned the most when events did not play out as planned. While some of the cases terminated successfully, others did not. This is not a commentary on the author or the author's skill level. Everyone has cases (sometimes too many) that do not turn out as planned. We chose cases based on one simple criterion: did it provide the best possible hope for practice education. We asked authors to teach practice by considering cases that were interesting and difficult, regardless of outcome. We did not want the Casebook to become simply a vehicle to promote practice brilliance.

Mostly, we wanted this text to differ from other casebooks, because we were unsatisfied with casebooks as teaching tools. As part of the process of planning our Casebooks, we reviewed other casebooks and discussed with our graduate and undergraduate students approaches that best facilitated learning in the classroom. We discovered that many students were also dissatisfied with a casebook approach to education, for a variety of reasons. Below, we briefly address what our students told us about casebooks in general.

1. *Linear presentation.* One of the most significant problems involves case presentation. Generally, this involves two issues: linearity and brevity. Most written case studies give students the impression that practice actually proceeds smoothly, orderly, and in a sequential manner. These cases often leave students believing—or expecting—that clinical decisions are made beforehand and that practice normally proceeds as planned. In other words, students often enter the field believing that casework follows an *"A, leads to B, leads to C, leads to clients living happily ever after"* approach.

Experienced practitioners know better. In over 40 years of combined social work practice in a variety of settings, we have learned—often the "hard way"—that the opposite is true. We rarely, if ever, had a case proceed sequentially, whether our client is an individual, couple, family, group, community, or classroom. That is, the process of engagement (including cultural competence), assessment, treatment planning, intervention, and follow-up occur in a circular manner, rooted in the client's social, physical, and cultural context, and includes consideration of the practitioner, his or her organization, and the laws and policies that affect and/or determine the boundaries of social work practice and treatment funding.

Practice evolves in discontinuous cycles over time, including time-limited treatments mandated by the managed care system. Therefore, real-life clinical practice—just as in all developing human relationships—seems to consistently require stops and starts, take wrong-turns, and even, in some cases, require "do-overs." While the goal of competent practice is to facilitate an orderly helping process that includes planned change (Timberlake, Farber, & Sabatino, 2002), practice, as an orderly process, is more often a goal (or a myth) than planned certainty. Given the linearity of case presentations discussed above, readers are often left without an appreciation or understanding of practice as process.

Additionally, many of the case presentation texts we reviewed provided "hard" client data and asked students to develop treatment plans based on this data. Yet, as any experienced practitioner knows, the difficulty in practice occurs during engagement and data collection. The usual case approach often overlooks this important element of practice. While a book format limits process writing, we believe that the case format we devised here brings students closer to the "real thing."

2. *Little focus on client engagement.*   As we like to remind students, there are two words in the title of our profession: social and work. In order for the "work" to be successful, students must learn to master the "social"—primarily, client engagement and relationship building. Social work practice is relationship based (Saleebey, 2002) and, from our perspective, relies more on the processes involved in relationship building and client engagement than technical intervention skills (Johnson, 2004). Successful practice is often rooted more in the ability of practitioners to develop open and trusting relationships with client(s) than on their ability to employ specific methods of intervention (Johnson, 2004).

Yet, this critically important element of practice often goes understated or ignored. Some texts even assume that engagement skills somehow exist before learning about practice. We find this true in casebooks and primary practice texts as well. When it is discussed, engagement and relationship building is presented as a technical process that also proceeds in linear fashion. Our experience with students, employees, and practitioner/trainees over the last two decades suggests that it is wrong to assume that students and/or practitioners have competent engagement or relationship building skills. From our perspective, developing a professional relationship that involves trust and openness, where clients feel safe to dialogue about the most intimate and sometimes embarrassing events in their lives, is the primary responsibility of the practitioner, and often spells the difference between positive and negative client outcome (Johnson, 2004; Miller & Rollnick, 2002; Harper & Lantz, 1996). Hence, each case presentation tries to provide a sense of this difficult and often elusive process and some of the ways that the authors overcame challenges to the culturally competent client engagement process.

Target Audience

Our target audience for this text, and the others in the series, are advanced undergraduate as well as foundation and advanced graduate students in social work and other helping disciplines. We have tested our approach with students at several different points in their education. We find that the casebooks can be used as:

- An adjunct learning tool for undergraduates preparing for or already involved in their field practicum.
- Practice education and training for foundation-level graduate students in practice theory and/or methods courses.
- An adjunct learning tool for second-year graduate students in field practicum.
- An adjunct learning tool for undergraduate and/or graduate students in any practice courses pertaining to specific populations.

While we are social work educators, we believe the casebooks will be useful in social work and other disciplines in the human services, including counseling psychology, counseling, mental health, psychology, and specialty disciplines such as marriage and family therapy, substance abuse, and mental health degree or certificate programs. Any educational or training program designed to prepare students to work with clients in a helping capacity may find the casebooks useful as a learning tool.

Structure of Cases

We organized the case studies to maximize critical thinking, the use of professional literature, evidenced-based practice knowledge, and classroom discussion in the learning process. At various points throughout each case, we comment on issues and/or dilemmas highlighted by the case. Our comments always end with a series of questions designed to focus student learning by calling on their ability to find and evaluate evidence from the professional literature and through classroom discussion. We ask students to collect evidence on different sides of an issue, evaluate that evidence, and develop a professional position that they can defend in writing and/or discussion with other students in the classroom or seminar setting.

We hope that you find the cases and our format as instructive and helpful in your courses as we have in ours. We have field-tested our format in courses at our university, finding that students respond well to the length, depth, and rigor of the case presentations. Universally, students report that the case materials were an important part of their overall learning process.

Organization of the Text

We organized this text to maximize its utility in any course. Chapter 1 provides an overview of the Advanced Multi-Systemic (AMS) practice approach. We provide this as one potential organizing tool for students to use while reading and evaluating the subsequent cases. This chapter offers students an organized and systematic framework to use when analyzing cases and/or formulating narrative assessments, treatment, and intervention plans. Our intent is to provide a helpful tool, not make a political statement about the efficacy or popularity of one practice framework versus others. In fact, we invite faculty and students to apply whatever practice framework they wish when working the cases.

In Chapter 2, author *Jan Wrenn, ACSW, MSW* presents her work with **Alice and Eric,** a single-parent family suffering with grief and loss since the death of Alice's father/Eric's grandfather. This case is an excellent example of working with children and parents through the grief process.

In Chapter 3, *Sharyl St. John, MSW, CSW* presents a case involving an adult woman having significant difficulties in her family. In a case entitled **Dee,** St. John takes us through her client's treatment as she proceeds from the initial intake to termination. Along the way, readers get to see how skilled practitioners use systems interventions to help an individual, and the role of medication in treatment.

In Chapter 4, *Rosalyn D. Baker, MSW, CSW* offers an interesting case involving marital therapy, depression, the use of medication, and a revised diagnosis based on the lack of clinical progress. In a case entitled **Dan and Ellen,** Baker takes readers through a difficult case that involves marital problems, serious mental disorders, domestic violence, and the fluctuations involved in treating serious mental disorders in outpatient settings.

The final chapter, **Carletta,** presents *Patricia Stowe Bolea's, Ph.D., ACSW* work with an adolescent girl suffering from a chronic illness that is trying to manage her personal growth and development. Dr. Stowe Bolea also works with the family in an interesting example of the power of religion and culture in people's lives.

Acknowledgments

We would like to thank the contributors to this text, Jan Wrenn, Sharyl St. John, Rosalyn Baker, and Patricia Stowe Bolea for their willingness to allow their work to be challenged and discussed in a public venue. We would also like to thank Patricia Quinlin and her people at Allyn and Bacon for their faith in the Casebook Series and in our ability to manage fourteen manuscripts at once. Additionally, we have to thank all of our students and student assistants that served as "guinea pigs" for our case studies. Their willingness to provide honest feedback contributes mightily to this series.

Jerry L. Johnson—I want to thank my wife, Cheryl, for her support and willingness to give me the time and encouragement to write and edit. I also owe a debt of gratitude to my dear friend Hope, for being there when I need you the most.

George Grant, Jr.—I want to thank Dean Rodney Mulder and Dr. Elaine Schott for their insight, encouragement, and support during this process. I also thank Dr. Julius Franks and Professor Daniel Groce for their intellectual discourse and unwavering support.

Contributors

The Editors

Jerry L. Johnson, Ph.D., MSW is an Associate Professor in the School of Social Work at Grand Valley State University in Grand Rapids, Michigan. He received his MSW from Grand Valley State University and his Ph.D. in sociology from Western Michigan University. Johnson has been in social work for more than 20 years as a practitioner, supervisor, administrator, consultant, teacher, and trainer. He was the recipient of two Fulbright Scholarship awards to Albania in 1998–99 and 2000–01. In addition to teaching and writing, Johnson serves in various consulting capacities in countries such as Albania and Armenia. He is the author of two previous books, *Crossing Borders—Confronting History: Intercultural Adjustment in a Post-Cold War World* (2000, Rowan and Littlefield) and *Fundamentals of Substance Abuse Practice* (2004, Wadsworth Brooks/Cole).

George Grant, Jr., Ph.D., MSW is an Associate Professor in the School of Social Work at Grand Valley State University in Grand Rapids, Michigan. Grant, Jr., also serves as the Director of Grand Valley State University's BSW Program. He received his MSW from Grand Valley State University and Ph.D. in sociology from Western Michigan University. Grant, Jr., has a long and distinguished career as practitioner, administrator, consultant, teacher, and trainer in social work, primarily in fields dedicated to Child Welfare.

Contributors

Jan Wrenn, ACSW, MSW has taught in the social work department at Andrews University since 1996, teaching both BSW and MSW students. She also served as the BSW Program Director for three years. Prior to teaching, Jan worked in an outpatient clinical social work position, where she counseled children, adolescents, adults, couples, and families. She received her MSW from The University of Michigan.

Sharyl St. John, MSW, CSW has an MSW with a holistic health specialty. She has three years of experience performing clinical social work in an outpatient setting. St. John presently works for a Community Mental Health agency. She also provides outpatient services for Woodlands Behavioral Healthcare in Cass County, Michigan, and teaches at Kalamazoo Valley Community College in Kalamazoo, Michigan.

Rosalyn D. Baker, MSW, CSW graduated with her BSW and Secondary Teaching Certificate in 1978 and her MSW in 1983. She is a Michigan State Certified Social Worker, Licensed Marriage and Family Therapist, Master Addiction Counselor, and Neurotherapist. She maintains a private practice in Grand Rapids, Michigan, treating individuals, couples, and families. Her clinical focus includes the treatment of depression, anxiety, and eating disorders.

Patricia Stow Bolea, Ph.D., ACSW is an Associate Professor in the School of Social Work at Grand Valley State University. She received her B.S. degree from Ball State University, her MSW from Indiana University, and her Ph.D. from Michigan State University.

Bibliography _____

Cournoyer, B. R. (2004). *The evidence-based social work skills book.* Boston: Allyn and Bacon.

Gibbs, L. E. (2003). *Evidence-based practice for the helping professions: A practical guide with integrated multimedia.* Pacific Grove, CA: Brooks/Cole.

Harper, K. V., & Lantz, J. (1996). *Cross-cultural practice: Social work practice with diverse populations.* Chicago: Lyceum Books.

Johnson, J. L. (2004). *Fundamentals of substance abuse practice.* Pacific Grove, CA: Brooks/Cole.

Miller, W. R., & Rollnick, S. (2002). *Motivational interviewing: Preparing people to change addictive behavior* (2nd ed.). New York: Guilford Press.

Saleebey, D. (2002). *The strengths perspective in social work practice* (3rd ed.). Boston: Allyn and Bacon.

Timberlake, E. M., Farber, M. Z., & Sabatino, C. A. (2002). *The general method of social work practice: McMahon's generalist perspective* (4th ed.). Boston: Allyn and Bacon.

A Multi-Systemic Approach to Practice

Jerry L. Johnson & George Grant, Jr.

This is a practice-oriented text, designed to build practice skills with individuals, families, and groups. We intend to provide you the opportunity to study the process involved in treating real cases from the caseloads of experienced practitioners. Unlike other casebooks, we include fewer cases, but provide substantially more detail in hopes of providing a realistic look into the thinking, planning, and approach of the practitioners/authors. We challenge you to study the authors' thinking and methods to understand their approach and then use critical thinking skills and the knowledge you have gained in your education and practice to propose alternative ways of treating the same clients. In other words, what would your course of action be if you were the primary practitioner responsible for these cases? Our hope is that this text provides a worthwhile and rigorous experience studying real cases as they progressed in practice.

Before proceeding to the cases, we include this chapter as an introduction to the Advanced Multi-Systemic (AMS) practice perspective. We decided to present this introduction with two primary goals in mind. First, we want you to use the information contained in this chapter to help assess and analyze the cases in this text. You will have the opportunity to complete a multi-systemic assessment, diagnoses, treatment, and intervention plan for each case. This chapter will provide the theoretical and practical basis for this exercise. Second, we hope you find that AMS makes conceptualizing cases clearer in your practice environment. We do not suggest that AMS is the only way, or even the best way for every practitioner to conceptualize cases. We simply know, through experience, that AMS is an effective way to think about practice with client-systems of all sizes and configurations. While there are many approaches to practice, AMS offers an effective way to place clinical decisions in the context of client lives and experiences, making engagement and treatment productive for clients and practitioners.

Advanced Multi-Systemic (AMS) Practice

Sociological Roots

> Whether the point of interest is a great power state or a minor literary mood, a family, a prison, and a creed—these are the kinds of questions the best social analysts have asked. They are the intellectual pivots of classic studies of (person) in society—and they are the questions inevitably raised by any mind possessing the sociological imagination. For that imagination is the capacity to shift from one perspective to another—from the political to the psychological; from examination of a single family to comparative assessment of the national budgets of the world; from the theological school to the military establishment; from considerations of an oil industry to studies of contemporary poetry. It is the capacity to range from the most impersonal and remote transformations to the most intimate features of the human self—and see the relations between the two. Back of its use is always the urge to know the social and historical meaning of the individual in the society and in the period in which he (or she) has his quality and his (or her) being. (Mills, 1959, p. 7; parentheses added)

Above, sociologist C. Wright Mills provided a seminal description of the sociological imagination. As it turns out, Mills's sociological imagination is also an apt description of AMS. Mills believed that linking people's "private troubles" to "public issues" (p. 2) was the most effective way to understand people and their issues, by placing them in historical context. It forces investigators to contextualize individuals and families in the framework of the larger social, political, economic, and historical environments in which they live. Ironically, this is also the goal of social work practice (Germain & Gitterman, 1996; Longres, 2000). Going further, Mills (1959) stated:

> We have come to know that every individual lives, from one generation to the next, in some society; that he (or she) lives out a biography, and that he (or she) lives it out within some historical sequence. By the fact of his (or her) living he (or she) contributes, however minutely, to the shaping of this society and to the course of its history, even as he (or she) is made by society and by its historical push and shove. (p. 6)

Again, Mills was not speaking as a social worker. He was an influential sociologist, speaking about a method of social research. In *The Sociological Imagination,* Mills (1959) proposed this as a method to understand the links between people, their daily lives, and their multi-systemic environment. Yet, while laying the theoretical groundwork for social research, Mills also provided the theoretical foundation for an effective approach to social work practice. We find four relevant points in *The Sociological Imagination* that translate directly to social work practice.

1. It is crucial to recognize the relationships between people's personal issues and strengths (private troubles) and the issues (political, economic, social, historical, and legal) and strengths of the multi-systemic environment (public issues) in which people live daily and across their life span. A multi-systemic understanding includes recognizing and integrating issues and strengths at the micro (individual, family, extended kin, etc.), mezzo (local community), and macro (state, region, national, and international policy, laws, political, economic, and social) levels during client engagement, assessment, treatment, follow-up, and evaluation of practice.

2. This depth of understanding (by social workers and, especially, clients) can lead to change in people's lives. We speak here about second-order change, or, significant change that makes a long-term difference in people's lives; change that helps people view themselves differently in relationship to their world. This level of change becomes possible when people make multi-systemic links in a way that makes sense to them (Freire, 1993). In other words, clients become "empowered" to change when they understand their life in the context of their world and realize that they have previously unforeseen or unimagined choices in how they live, think, believe, and act.

3. Any assessment and/or clinical diagnoses that exclude multi-systemic links do not provide a holistic picture of people's lives, their troubles, and/or strengths. In sociology, this leads to a reductionist view of people and society, while in social work it reduces the likelihood that services will be provided (or received by clients) in a way that addresses client problems and utilizes client strengths in a meaningful way. The opportunity for change is reduced whenever client life history is overlooked because it does not fit, or is not called for, in a practitioner's preferred method of helping, or because of shortcuts many people believe are needed in a managed care environment. One cannot learn too much about their clients, their lives, and their attitudes, beliefs, and values as it relates to the private troubles presented in treatment.

4. Inherent in AMS and foundational to achieving all that was discussed above relies on practitioners being able to rapidly develop rapport with clients that leads to engagement in treatment. In this text, client engagement

> . . . occurs when you develop, in collaboration with clients, a trusting and open professional relationship that promotes hope and presents viable prospects for change. Successful engagement occurs when you create a social context in which vulnerable people (who often hold jaded attitudes toward helping professionals) can share their innermost feelings, as well as their most embarrassing and shameful behavior with you, a *total stranger.* (Johnson, 2004, p. 93; emphasis in original)

AMS Overview

First, we should define two important terms that comprise AMS. Understanding these terms is important, because they provide the foundation for understanding the language and concepts used throughout the remainder of this chapter.

    1. Advanced.   According to Derezotes (2000), "the most advanced theory is also the most inclusive" (p. viii). AMS is advanced because it is inclusive. It requires responsible practitioners, in positions of responsibility (perhaps as solo practitioners), to acquire a depth of knowledge, skills, and self-awareness that allows for an inclusive application of knowledge acquired in the areas of human behavior in the social environment, social welfare policy, social research and practice evaluation, and multiple practice methods and approaches in service of clients and client systems of various sizes, types, and configurations.

    AMS practitioners are expected to have the most inclusive preparation possible, "both the broad generalist base of knowledge, skills, and values and an in-depth proficiency in practice . . . with selected social work methods and populations" (Derezotes, 2000, p. xii). Hence, advanced practitioners are well-trained and, with in-depth knowledge, are often in positions of being responsible for clients as primary practitioners. They are afforded the responsibility for engaging, assessing, intervening, and evaluating practice, ensuring that clients are ethically treated in a way that is culturally competent and respectful of their client's worldview. In other words, AMS practitioners develop the knowledge, skills, and values needed to be leaders in their organizations, communities, the social work profession, and especially in the treatment of their clients. The remainder of this chapter explains why AMS is an advanced approach to practice.

    2. Multi-systemic.   From the earliest moments in their education, social workers learn a systems perspective that emphasizes the connectedness between people and their problems to the complex interrelationships that exist in their client's world (Timberlake, Farber, & Sabatino, 2002). To explain these connections, systems theory emphasizes three important concepts: wholeness, relationships, and homeostasis. Wholeness refers to the notion that the various parts or elements (subsystem) of a system interact to form a whole that best describes the system in question. This concept asserts that no system can be understood or explained unless the connectedness of the subsystems to the whole are understood or explained. In other words, the whole is greater than the sum of its parts. Moreover, systems theory also posits that change in one subsystem will affect change in the system as a whole.

    In terms of systems theory, relationship refers to the patterns of interaction and overall structures that exist within and between subsystems. The nature of these relationships is more important than the system itself. That is, when trying to understand or explain a system (individual, family, or organization, etc.), how subsystems connect through relationships, the characteristics of the relationships between subsystems, and how the subsystems interact provide clues to understanding the system as a whole. Hence, the application of systems theory is primarily based on understanding relationships. As someone once said about systems theory, in systems problems occur between people and subsystems (relationships), not "in" them. People's internal problems relate to the nature of the relationships in the systems where they live and interact.

Homeostasis refers to the notion that most living systems work to maintain and preserve the existing system, or the status quo. For example, family members often assume roles that serve to protect and maintain family stability, often at the expense of "needed" change. The same can be said for organizations or groups. The natural tendency toward homeostasis in systems represents what we call the "dilemma of change" (Johnson, 2004). This can best be described as the apparent conflict, or what appears to be client resistance or lack of motivation, that often occurs when clients approach moments of significant change. Systems of all types and configurations struggle with the dilemma of change: should they change to the unknown or remain the same, even if the status quo is unhealthy or unproductive? Put differently, systems strive for stability, even at the expense of health and well-being of individual members and/or the system itself.

What do we mean then, by the term *multi-systemic*? Clients (individuals, families, etc.) are systems that interact with a number of different systems simultaneously. These systems exist and interact at multiple levels, ranging from the micro level (individual and families), the mezzo level (local community, institutions, organizations, the practitioner and their agency, etc.), to the macro level (culture, laws and policy, politics, oppression and discrimination, international events, etc.). How these various systems come together, interact, and adapt, along with the relationships that exist within and between each system work together to comprise the "whole" that is the client, or client-system. In practice, the client (individual, couple, family, etc.) is not the "system," but one of many interacting subsystems in a maze of other subsystems constantly interacting to create the system—the client plus elements from multiple subsystems at each level. It would be a mistake to view the client as the whole system. They are but one facet of a multi-dimensional and multi-level system comprised of the client and various other subsystems at the micro, mezzo, and macro levels.

Therefore, the term *multi-systemic* refers to the nature of a system comprised of the various multi-level subsystems described above. A multi-systemic perspective recognizes that clients are *one part or subsystem* in relationship with other subsystemic influences occurring on different levels. This level of understanding—the system as the whole produced through multi-systemic subsystem interactions—is the main unit of investigation for practice. As stated above, it is narrow to consider the client as a functioning independent system with peripheral involvement with other systems existing outside of their intimate world. These issues and relationships work together to help shape and mold the client who in turn, shapes and molds his or her relationship to the other subsystems. Yet, the person-of-the-client is but one part of the system in question during practice.

AMS provides an organized framework for gathering, conceptualizing, and analyzing multi-systemic client data and for proceeding with the helping process. It defines the difference between social work and other disciplines in the helping professions at the level of theory and practice. How, you ask? Unlike other professional disciplines that tend to focus on one or a few domains (i.e., psychology, medicine, etc.), AMS provides a comprehensive and holistic "picture" of clients or client-systems in the context of their environment by considering information about multiple personal and systemic domains simultaneously.

Resting on the generalist foundation taught in all Council on Social Work Education (CSWE) accredited undergraduate and foundation-level graduate programs, AMS requires practitioners to contextualize client issues in the context of the multiple interactions that occur between the client/client-system and the social, economic, legal, political, and physical environment in which the client lives. It is a unifying perspective based in the client's life, history, and culture that guides the process of collecting and analyzing client life information and intervening to promote personal choice through a comprehensive, multi-systemic framework. Beginning with culturally competent client engagement, a comprehensive multi-systemic assessment points toward a holistically based treatment plan that requires practitioners to select and utilize appropriate practice theories, models, and methods—or combinations thereof—that best fit the client's unique circumstances and needs.

AMS is not a practice theory, model, or method itself. It is a perspective or framework for conceptualizing client-systems. It relies on the practitioner's ability to use a variety of theories, models, and methods, and to incorporate knowledge from human behavior, social policy, research/evaluation, and practice into his or her routine approach with clients. For example, an AMS practitioner will have the skills to apply different approaches to individual treatment (client-centered, cognitive-behavioral, etc.), family treatment (structural, narrative, Bowenian, etc.), work with couples, in groups, arrange for specialized care if needed, and, as an advocate on behalf of their client. It may also require practitioners to treat clients in a multi-modal approach (i.e., individual and group treatments simultaneously).

Practitioners not only must know how to apply different approaches but also how to determine, primarily through the early engagement and assessment process, which theory, model, or approach (direct or indirect, for example) would work best for a particular client. Hence, successful practice using AMS relies heavily on the practitioner's ability to competently engage and multi-systemically assess client problems and strengths. Practitioners must simultaneously develop a sense of their client's personal interaction and relationship style—especially related to how they relate to authority figures—when determining which approach would best suit the client. For example, a reserved, quiet, or thoughtful client or someone who lacks assertiveness may not be well served by a directive, confrontational approach, regardless of the practitioner's preference. Moreover, AMS practitioners rely on professional practice research and outcome studies to help determine which approach or intervention package might work best for particular clients and/or client-systems. AMS expects practitioners to know how to find and evaluate practice research in their practice areas or specialties.

Elements of the Advanced Multi-Systemic Approach to Social Work Practice

The advanced multi-systemic approach entails the following seven distinct, yet integrated elements of theory and practice. Each is explained below.

Ecological Systems Perspective

One important subcategory of systems therapy for social work is the ecological systems perspective. This perspective combines important concepts from the science of ecology and general systems theory into a way of viewing client problems and strengths in social work practice. In recent years, it has become the prevailing perspective for social work practice (Miley, O'Melia, & DuBois, 2004). The ecological systems perspective—sometimes referred to as the ecosystems perspective—is a useful metaphor for guiding social workers as they think about cases (Germain & Gitterman, 1980).

Ecology focuses on how subsystems work together and adapt. In ecology, adaptation is "a dynamic process between people and their environments as people grow, achieve competence, and make contributions to others" (Greif, 1986, p. 225). Insight from ecology leads to an analysis of how people fit within their environment and what adaptations are made in the fit between people and their environments. Problems develop as a function of inadequate or improper adaptation or fit between people and their environments.

General systems theory focuses on how human systems interact. It focuses specifically on how people grow, survive, change, and achieve stability or instability in the complex world of multiple systemic interactions (Miley, O'Melia, & DuBois, 2004). General systems theory has contributed significantly to the growth of the family therapy field and to how social workers understand their clients.

Together, ecology and general systems theory evolved into what social workers know as the ecological systems perspective. The ecological systems perspective provides a systemic framework for understanding the many ways that persons and environments interact. Accordingly, individuals and their individual circumstances can be understood in the context of these interactions. The ecological systems perspective provides an important part of the foundation for AMS. Miley, O'Melia, and DuBois (2004) provide an excellent summary of the ecological systems perspective. They suggest that it

1. Presents a dynamic view of human beings as system interactions in context.
2. Emphasizes the significance of human system interactions.
3. Traces how human behavior and interaction develop over time in response to internal and external forces.
4. Describes current behavior as an adaptive fit of "persons in situations."
5. Conceptualizes all interaction as adaptive or logical in context.
6. Reveals multiple options for change within persons, their social groups, and in their social and physical environments (p. 33).

Social Constructionism

To maintain AMS as an inclusive practice approach, we need to build on the ecological systems perspective by including ideas derived from social constructionism. Social constructionism builds on the ecological systems perspective by introducing ideas about how people define themselves and their environment. Social constructionism also, by definition, introduces the role of culture in the meaning people give to themselves and other systems in their multi-systemic environments. The ecological systems perspective discusses relationships at the systemic level. Social constructionism introduces meaning and value into the equation, allowing for a deeper understanding and appreciation of the nature of multi-systemic relationships and adaptations.

Usually, people assume that reality is something "out there" that hits them in the face, something that independently exists, and people must learn to "deal with it." Social constructionism posits something different. Evolving as a critique of the "one reality" belief system, social constructionism points out that the world is comprised of multiple realities. People define their own reality and then live within those definitions. Accordingly, the definition of reality will be different for everyone. Hence, social constructionism deals primarily with meaning, or the systemic processes by which people come to define themselves in their social world. As sociologist W. I. Thomas said, in what has become known as the Thomas Theorem, "If people define situations as real, they are real in their consequences."

For example, some people believe that they can influence the way computerized slot machines pay out winnings by the way they sit, the feeling they get from the machine as they look at it in the casino, by the clothes they are wearing, or by how they trigger the machine, either by pushing the button or pulling the handle. Likewise, many athletes believe that a particular article of clothing, a routine for getting dressed, and/or a certain pregame meal dictates the quality of their athletic prowess that day.

Illogical to most people, the belief that they can influence a computerized machine, that the machine emits feelings, or that an article of clothing dictates athletic prowess is real to some people. For these people, their beliefs influence the way they live. Perhaps you have ideas or "superstitions" that you believe influence how your life goes on a particular day. This is a common occurrence. These people are not necessarily out of touch with objective reality. While people may know, at some level, that slot machines pay according to preset, computerized odds or that athletic prowess has nothing to do with dressing routines, the belief systems continue. What dictates the behavior and beliefs discussed above or in daily "superstitutions" have nothing to do with objective reality and everything to do with people's subjective reality. Subjective reality—or a person's learned definition of the situation—overrides objectivity and helps determine how people behave and/or what they believe.

While these examples may be simplistic, according to social constructionism, the same processes influence everyone—always. In practice, understanding that people's behavior does not depend on the objective existence of something, but on their subjective interpretation of it, is crucial to effective application of AMS. This knowledge is most helpful during client engagement. If practitioners remember that practice is about understanding people's perceptions and not objective reality, they reduce the likelihood that clients will feel misunderstood, there will be fewer disagreements, and it becomes easier to avoid the trap of defining normal behavior as client resistance or a diagnosable mental disorder. This perspective contributes to a professional relationship based in the client's life and belief systems, is consistent with his or her worldview, and one that is culturally appropriate for the client. Being mindful that the definitions people learn from their culture underlies not only what they do but also what they perceive, feel, and think places practitioners on the correct path to "start where the client is." Social constructionism emphasizes the cultural uniqueness of each client and/or client-system and the need to understand each client and/or client-system in her own context and belief systems, not the practitioner's context or belief systems.

Social constructionism also posits that different people attribute different meaning to the same events, because the interactional contexts and the way individuals interpret these contexts are different for everyone, even within the same family or community. One cannot assume that people raised in the same family will define their social world similarly. Individuals, in the context of their environments, derive meaning through a complex process of individual interpretation. This is how siblings from the same family can be so different, almost as if they did not grow up in the same family. For example, the sound of gunfire in the middle of the night may be frightening or normal, depending upon where a person resides and what is routine and accepted in his specific environment. Moreover, simply because some members of a family or community understand nightly gunfire as normal does not mean that others in the same family or community will feel the same.

Additionally, social constructionism examines how people construct meaning with language and established or evolving cultural beliefs. For example, alcohol consumption is defined as problematic depending upon how the concept of "alcohol problem" is socially constructed in specific environments. Clients from so-called drinking cultures may define drinking six alcoholic drinks daily as normal, while someone from a different cultural background may see this level of consumption as problematic. One of the authors worked in Russia and found an issue that demonstrates this point explicitly. Colleagues in Russia stated rather emphatically that consuming one "bottle" (approximately a U.S. pint) of vodka per day was acceptable and normal. People that consume more than one bottle per day were defined as having a drinking problem. The same level of consumption in the United States would be considered by most as clear evidence of problem drinking.

Biopsychosocial Perspective

Alone, the ecological systems perspective, even with the addition of social constructionism, does not provide the basis for the holistic understanding required by AMS. While it provides a multi-systemic lens, the ecological systems perspective focuses mostly on externals. That is, how people interact and adapt to their environments and how environments interact and adapt to people. Yet, much of what practitioners consider "clinical" focuses on "internals" or human psychological and emotional functioning. Therefore, the ecological systems perspective provides only one part of the holistic picture required by the advanced multi-systemic approach. By adding the biopsychosocial perspective, practitioners can consider the internal workings of human beings to help explain how external and internal subsystems interact.

What is the biopsychosocial perspective? It is a theoretical perspective that considers how human biological, psychological, and social-functioning subsystems interact to account for how people live in their environment. Similar to social systems, human beings are also multidimensional systems comprised of multiple subsystems constantly interacting in their environment, the human body. The biopsychosocial perspective applies multi-systemic thinking to individual human beings.

Several elements comprise the biopsychosocial perspective. Longres (2000) identifies two dimensions of individual functioning, the biophysical and the psychological; subdividing the psychological into three subdimensions: the cognitive, affective, and behavioral. Elsewhere, we added the spiritual/existential dimension to this conception (Johnson, 2004). Understanding how the biological, psychological, spiritual and existential, and social subsystems interact is instrumental in developing an appreciation of how individuals influence and are influenced by their social systemic environments. Realizing that each of these dimensions interacts with external social and environmental systems allow practitioners to enlarge their frame of reference, leading to a more holistic multi-systemic view of clients and client-systems.

Strengths/Empowerment Perspective

Over the last few years, the strengths perspective has emerged as an important part of social work theory and practice. The strengths perspective represents a significant change in how social workers conceptualize clients and client-systems. According to Saleebey (2002), it is "a versatile practice approach, relying heavily on ingenuity and creativity. . . . Rather than focusing on problems, your eye turns toward possibility" (p. 1). Strengths-based practitioners believe in the power of possibility and hope in helping people overcome problems by focusing on, locating, and supporting existing personal or systemic strengths and resiliencies. The strengths perspective is based on the belief that people, regardless of the severity of their problems, have the capabilities and resources to play an active role in helping solve their own problems. The practitioner's role is to engage clients in a way that unleashes these capabilities and resources toward solving problems and changing lives.

Empowerment

Any discussion of strengths-based approaches must also consider empowerment as an instrumental element of the approach. Empowerment, as a term in social work, has evolved over the years. We choose a definition of empowerment that focuses on power; internal, interpersonal, and environmental (Parsons, Gutierrez, & Cox, 1998). According to Parsons, Gutierrez, and Cox (1998),

> In its most positive sense, power is (1) the ability to influence the course of one's life, (2) an expression of self worth, (3) the capacity to work with others to control aspects of public life, and (4) access to the mechanisms of public decision making. When used negatively, though, it can also block opportunities for stigmatized groups, exclude others and their concerns from decision making, and be a way to control others. (p. 8)

Hence, empowerment in practice is a process (Parsons, Gutierrez, and Cox, 1998) firmly grounded in ecological systems and strength-based approaches that focus on gaining power by individuals, families, groups, organizations, or communities. It is based on two related assumptions: (1) all human beings are potentially competent, even in extremely challenging situations, and (2) all human beings are subject to various degrees of powerlessness (Cox & Parsons, 1994, p. 17) and oppression (Freire, 1993). People internalize their sense of powerlessness and oppression in a way that their definition of self in the world is limited, often eliminating any notion that they can act in their own behalf in a positive manner.

An empowerment approach makes practical connections between power and powerlessness. It illuminates how these factors interact to influence clients in their daily life. Empowerment is not achieved through a single intervention, nor is it something that can be "done" to another. Empowerment does not occur through neglect or by simply giving responsibility for life and well-being to the poor or troubled, allowing them to be "free" from government regulation, support, or professional assistance. In other words, empowerment of disenfranchised groups does not occur simply by dismantling systems (such as the welfare system) to allow these groups or individuals to take responsibility for themselves. Hence, empowerment does not preclude helping.

Consistent with our definition, empowerment develops through the approach taken toward helping, not the act of helping itself. Empowerment is a sense of gained or regained power that someone attains in their life that provides the foundation for change in the short term, and stimulates belief in their ability to positively influence their lives over the long term. Empowerment occurs as a function of the long-term approach of the practitioner and the professional relationship developed between practitioner and client. One cannot provide an empowering context through a constant focus on problems, deficits, inadequacies, negative labeling, and dependency.

The Power of Choice

Choice is an instrumental part of strengths-based and empowerment approaches, by recognizing that people, because of inherent strengths and capabilities, can make informed choices about their lives, just like people who are not clients. Practitioners work toward offering people choices about how they define their lives and problems, the extent to which they want to address their problems, and the means or mechanisms through which change should occur. Clients become active and instrumental partners in the helping process. They are not passive vessels, waiting for practitioners to "change them" through some crafty intervention or technique.

We are not talking about the false choices sometimes given to clients by practitioners. For example, clients with substance abuse problems are often told that they must either abstain or leave treatment. Most practitioners ignore or use as evidence of denial, client requests to attempt so-called controlled use. If practitioners were interested in offering true choice, they would work with these clients toward their controlled-drinking goal in an effort to reduce the potential harm that may result from their use of substances (Johnson, 2004; van Wormer & Davis, 2003), even if the practitioner believes that controlled drinking is not possible. Abstinence would become the goal only when their clients choose to include it as a goal.

Client Engagement as Cultural Competence

Empowerment (choice) occurs through a process of culturally competent client engagement, created by identifying strengths, generating dialogue targeted at revealing the extent of people's oppression (Freire, 1993), and respecting their right to make informed choices in their lives. Accordingly, empowerment is the "transformation from individual and collective powerlessness to personal, political, and cultural power" (GlenMaye, 1998, p. 29), through a strengths-based relationship with a professional helper.

Successful application of AMS requires the ability to engage clients in open and trusting professional relationships. The skills needed to engage clients from different backgrounds and with different personal and cultural histories are what drives practice; what determines the difference between successful and unsuccessful practice. Advanced client engagement skills allow the practitioner to elicit in-depth, multi-systemic information in a dialogue between client and practitioner (Johnson, 2004), providing the foundation for strengths-based client empowerment leading to change.

Earlier, we defined client engagement as a mutual process occurring between clients and practitioners in a professional context, created by practitioners. In other words, creating the professional space and open atmosphere that allows engagement to flourish is the primary responsibility of the practitioner, not the client. Practitioners must have the skills and knowledge to adjust their approach toward specific clients and the client's cultural context and not *vice versa*. Clients do not adjust to us and our beliefs, values, and practices—we adjust to them. When that occurs, the foundation exists for client engagement. By definition, relationships of this nature must be performed in a culturally competent manner. Yet, what does this mean?

Over the last two decades, social work and other helping professions have been concerned with cultural competence in practice (Fong, 2001). Beginning in the late 1970s, the professional literature has been replete with ideas, definitions, and practice models designed to increase cultural awareness and promote culturally appropriate practice methods. Yet, despite the attention given to the issue, there remains confusion about how to define and teach culturally competent practice.

Structural and Historical Systems of Oppression: Who Holds the Power?

Often embedded in laws, policies, and social institutions are oppressive influences such as racism, sexism, homophobia, and classism, to name a few. These structural issues play a significant role in the lives of clients (through maltreatment and discrimination) and in social work practice. How people are treated (or how they internalize historical treatment of self, family, friends, and/or ancestors) shapes how they believe, think, and act in the present. Oppression affects how they perceive that others feel about them, how they view the world and their place in it, and how receptive they are to professional service providers. Therefore, culturally competent practice must consider the impact of structural systems of oppression and injustice on clients, their problems, strengths, and potential for change.

Oppression is a by-product of socially constructed notions of power, privilege, control, and hierarchies of difference. As stated above, it is created and maintained by differences in power. By definition, those who have power can force people to abide by the rules, standards, and actions the powerful deem worthwhile, mandatory, or acceptable. Those who hold power can enforce particular worldviews; deny equal access and opportunity to housing, employment, or health care; define right and wrong, normal and abnormal; and imprison, confine, and/or commit physical, emotional, or mental violence against the powerless (McLaren, 1995; Freire, 1993). Most importantly, power permits the holder to "set the very terms of power" (Appleby, 2001, p. 37). It defines the interaction between the oppressed and the oppressor, and between the social worker and client.

Social institutions and practices are developed and maintained by the dominant culture to meet *its* needs and maintain *its* power. Everything and everybody is judged and classified accordingly. Even when the majority culture develops programs or engages in helping activities, these efforts will not include measures that threaten the dominant group's position at the top of the social hierarchy (Freire, 1993). For example, Kozol (1991) wrote eloquently about how public schools fail by design, while Freire (1993) wrote about how state welfare and private charity provide short-term assistance while ensuring that there are not enough resources to lift people permanently out of poverty.

Oppression is neither an academic nor a theoretical consideration; it is not a faded relic of a bygone era. Racism did not end with the civil rights movement, and sexism was not eradicated by the feminist movement. Understanding how systems of oppression work in people's lives is of paramount importance for every individual and family seeking professional help, including those who belong to the *same* race, gender, and class as the practitioner. No two individuals, regardless of their personal demographics, experience the world in the same way. Often, clients are treated ineffectively by professional helpers who mistakenly believe that people who look or act the same will experience the world in similar ways. These workers base their assumptions about clients on stereotypic descriptions of culture, lifestyle, beliefs, and practices. They take group-level data (i.e., many African American adolescents join gangs because of broken families and poverty) and assume that *all* African American teenagers are gang members from single-parent families. Social work values and ethics demand a higher standard, one that compels us to go beyond stereotypes. Our job is to discover, understand, and utilize personal differences in the assessment and treatment process to benefit clients, not use differences as a way of limiting clients' potential for health and well-being.

We cannot accurately assess or treat people without considering the effects of oppression related to race, ethnicity, culture, sexual preference, gender, or physical/emotional status. We need to understand how oppression influences our clients' beliefs about problems and potential approaches to problem solving, and how it determines what kind of support they can expect to receive if they decide to seek help. For example, despite the widely held belief that chemical dependency is an equal opportunity disease (Gordon, 1993), it is clear that some people are more vulnerable than others. While some of the general themes of chemical dependency may appear universal, each client is unique. That is, an individual's dependency results from personal behavior, culture (including the history of one's culture), past experiences, and family interacting with larger social systems that provide opportunities or impose limits on the individual (Johnson, 2000).

Systems of oppression ensure unequal access to resources for certain individuals, families, and communities. However, while all oppressed people are similar in that they lack the power to define their place in the social hierarchy, oppression based on race, gender, sexual orientation, class, and other social factors is expressed in a variety of ways. Learning about cultural nuances is important in client assessment, treatment planning, and treatment (Lum, 1999). According to Pinderhughes (1989), there is no such thing as culture-free service delivery. Cultural differences between clients and social workers in terms of values, norms, beliefs, attitudes, lifestyles, and life opportunities affect every aspect of practice.

What Is Culture?

Many different concepts of culture are used in social work, sociology, and anthropology. Smelser (1992) considers culture a "system of patterned values, meanings, and beliefs that give cognitive structure to the world, provide a basis for coordinating and controlling human interactions, and constitute a link as the system is transmitted from one generation to another" (p. 11). Geertz (1973) regarded culture as simultaneously a product of and a guide to people searching for organized categories and interpretations that provide a meaningful experiential link to their social life. Building upon these two ideas, in this book we abide by the following definition of culture proposed elsewhere (Johnson, 2000):

> Culture is historical, bound up in traditions and practices passed through generations; memories of events—real or imagined—that define a people and their worldview. (Culture) is viewed as collective subjectivity, or a way of life adopted by a community that ultimately defines their worldview. (p. 121)

Consistent with this definition, the collective subjectivities called culture are pervasive forces in the way people interact, believe, think, feel, and act in their social world. Culture plays a significant role in shaping how people view the world. As a historical force, in part built on ideas, definitions, and events passed through generations, culture also defines people's level of social acceptance by the wider community; shapes how people live, think, and act; and influences how people perceive that others feel about them and how they view the world and their place in it. Thus, it is impossible to understand a client without grasping their cultural foundations.

Cultural Competence

As stated earlier, over the years many different ideas and definitions of what constitutes culturally competent practice have developed, as indicated by the growth of the professional literature since the late 1970s. To date, focus has primarily been placed in two areas: (1) the need for practitioners to be aware or their own cultural beliefs, ideas, and identities leading to cultural sensitivity, and (2) learning factual and descriptive information about various ethnic and racial groups based mostly on group-level survey data and analyses. Fong (2001) suggests that culture is often considered "tangential" to individual functioning and not central to the client's functioning (p. 5).

To address this issue, Fong (2001) builds on Lum's (1999) culturally competent practice model that focuses on four areas: (1) cultural awareness, (2) knowledge acquisition, (3) skill development, and (4) inductive learning. Besides inductive learning, Lum's model places focuses mainly on practitioners in perpetual self-awareness, gaining knowledge about cultures, and skill building. While these are important ideas for cultural competence, Fong (2001) calls for a shift in thinking and practice, "to provide a culturally competent service focused solely on the client rather than the social worker and what he or she brings to the awareness of ethnicity" (p. 5). Fong (2001) suggests an "extension" (p. 6) of Lum's model by turning the focus of each of the four elements away from the practitioner toward the client. For example, cultural awareness changes from a practitioner focus to "the social worker's understanding and the identification of the critical cultural values important to the client system and to themselves" (p. 6). This change allows Fong (2001) to remain consistent with the stated definition of culturally competent practice, insisting that practitioners

> . . . operating from an empowerment, strengths, and ecological framework, provide services, conduct assessments, and implement interventions that are reflective of the clients' cultural values and norms, congruent with their natural help-seeking behaviors, and inclusive of existing indigenous solutions. (p. 1)

While we agree with the idea that "to be culturally competent is to know the cultural values of the client system and to use them in planning and implementing services" (Fong, 2001, p. 6), we want to make this shift the main point of a culturally competent model of client engagement. That is, beyond what should or must occur, we believe that professional education and training must focus on the skills of culturally competent client engagement that are necessary to make this happen; a model that places individual client cultural information at the center of practice. We agree with Fong (2001) that having culturally sensitive or culturally aware practitioners is not nearly enough. Practitioner self-awareness and knowledge of different cultures does not constitute cultural competence. We strive to find a method for reaching this worthy goal.

The central issue revolves around practitioners participating in inductive learning and the skills of grounded theory. In other words, regardless of practitioner beliefs, awarenesses, or sensitivities, their job is to learn about and understand their client's world, and "ground" their theory of practice in the cultural context of their client. They develop a unique theory of human behavior in a multi-systemic context for every client. Culturally competent client engagement does not happen by assessing the extent to which client lives "fit" within existing theory and knowledge about reality, most of which is middle-class and Eurocentric at its core. Cultural competence (Johnson, 2004)

> . . . *begins* with learning about different cultures, races, personal circumstances, and structural mechanisms of oppression. It *occurs* when practitioners master the interpersonal skills needed to move beyond general descriptions of a specific culture or race to learn specific individual, family, group, or community interpretations of culture, ethnicity, and race. The culturally competent practitioner knows that within each culture are individually interpreted and practiced thoughts, beliefs, and behaviors that may or may not be consistent with group-level information. That is, there is tremendous diversity within groups, as well as between them. Individuals are unique unto themselves, not simply interchangeable members of a specific culture, ethnicity, or race who natu-

rally abide by the group-level norms often taught in graduate and undergraduate courses on human diversity. (p. 105)

Culturally competent client engagement revolves around the practitioner's ability to create a relationship, through the professional use of self, based in true dialogue (Freire, 1993; Johnson, 2004). We define dialogue as "a joint endeavor, developed between people (in this case, practitioner and client) that move clients from their current state of hopelessness to a more hopeful, motivated position in their world" (Johnson, 2004, p. 97). Elsewhere (Johnson, 2004), we detailed a model of culturally competent engagement based on Freire's (1993) definitions of oppression, communication, dialogue, practitioner self-work, and the ability to exhibit worldview respect, hope, humility, trust, and empathy.

To investigate culture in a competent manner is to take a comprehensive look into people's worldviews—to discover what they believe about the world and their place in it. It goes beyond race and ethnicity (although these are important issues) into how culture determines thoughts, feelings, and behaviors in daily life. This includes what culture says about people's problems; culturally appropriate strengths and resources; the impact of gender on these issues; and what it means to seek professional help (Leigh, 1998).

The larger questions to be answered are how clients uniquely and individually interpret their culture; how their beliefs, attitudes, and behaviors are shaped by that interpretation, and how these cultural beliefs and practices affect daily life and determine lifestyle in the context of the larger community. Additionally, based on their cultural membership, beliefs, and practices, practitioners need to discover the potential and real barriers faced by clients in the world. Many clients, because they are part of non-majority cultures, issues generated by social systems of oppression such as racism, sexism, homophobia, and ethnocentrism that expose them to limitations and barriers that others do not face.

What is the value of culturally competent client engagement? Helping clients discuss their attitudes, beliefs, and behaviors in the context of their culture—including their religious or spiritual belief systems—offers valuable information about their worldview, sense of social and spiritual connection, and/or practical involvement in their social world. Moreover, establishing connections between their unique interpretation of their culture and their daily life provides vital clues about people's belief systems, attitudes, expectations (social construction of reality), and explanation of behaviors that cannot be understood outside the context of their socially constructed interpretation of culture.

A Cautionary Note

It is easy to remember to ask about culture when clients are obviously different (i.e., different races, countries of origin, etc.). However, many practitioners forgo cultural investigation with clients they consider to have the same cultural background as the practitioner. For example, the search for differences between European-

Americans with Christian beliefs—if the social worker shares these characteristics—gets lost in mutual assumptions, based on the misguided belief that there are no important differences between them. The same is often true when clients and practitioners come from the same racial, cultural, or lifestyle backgrounds (i.e., African American practitioner and client, gay practitioner and gay client, etc.). Culturally competent practice means that practitioners are always interested in people's individual interpretation of their culture and their subjective definitions of reality, whether potential differences are readily apparent or not. Practitioners must be diligent to explore culture with clients who appear to be from the same background as the practitioner, just as they would with people who are obviously from different cultural, racial, ethnic, or religious backgrounds.

Multiple Theories and Methods

No single theory, model, or method is best suited to meet the needs of all clients (Miley, O'Melia, & DuBois, 2004). Consistent with this statement, one of the hallmarks of AMS is the expectation that practitioners must determine which theory, model, or method will best suit a particular client. Choosing from a range of approaches and interventions, AMS practitioners develop the skills and abilities to: (1) determine, based on the client's life, history, culture, and style, which treatment approach (theory and/or method) would best suit their needs and achieve the desired outcome, (2) determine which modality or modalities (individual, family, group treatment, etc.) will best meet the need of their clients, and (3) conduct treatment according to their informed clinical decisions.

Over the last 20 years or so, graduate social work education has trended toward practice specialization through concentration-based curricula. Many graduate schools of social work build on the generalist foundation by insisting that students focus on learning specific practice models or theories (disease, cognitive-behavioral, psychoanalysis, etc.) and/or specific practice methods (individual, family, group, etc.), often at the exclusion of other methods or models. For example, students often enter the field intent on doing therapy with individuals say, from a cognitive-behavioral approach only.

This trend encourages practitioners to believe that one approach or theory best represents the "Truth." Truth, in this sense, is the belief that one theory or approach works best for most people, most of the time. It helps create a practice scenario that leads practitioners to use their chosen approach with every client they treat. Therefore, practice becomes a process of the practitioner forcing clients to adjust to the practitioner's beliefs and expectations about the nature of problems, the course of treatment, and definition of positive versus negative outcomes. From this perspective, what is best for clients is determined by what the practitioner believes is best, not what clients believe is in their best interest.

Some practitioners take their belief in the Truth of a particular theory or method to extremes. They believe that one model or theory works best for all people, all the time. We found this to be common in the family therapy field, whereby some true believers insist that everyone needs family therapy—so that is all they offer. What's worse is that many of these same practitioners know and use only one particular family therapy theory and model. The "true believer" approach can cause problems, especially for clients. For example, when clients do not respond to treatment, instead of looking to other approaches, true believers simply prescribe more of the method that did not work in the first place. If a more intensive application of the method does not work, then the client's "lack of readiness" for treatment, resistance, or denial becomes the culprit. These practitioners usually give little thought to their practice approach or personal style and its impact on client "readiness" for treatment. They fail to examine the role their personal style, beliefs, attitudes, and practices have in creating the context that led to clients not succeeding in treatment.

Each practice theory and model has a relatively unique way of defining client problems, practitioner method and approach, interventions, and what constitutes successful outcome. For practitioners to believe that one theory or model is true, even if only for most people, they must believe in the universality of problems, methods and approaches, interventions, and successful outcome criteria. This contradicts the definition of theory. While being far from a concrete representation of the truth, a theory is a set of myths, expectations, guesses, and conjectures about what might be true (Best & Kellner, 1991). A theory is hypothetical; a set of ideas and explanations that need proving. No single theory can explain everything. According to Popper (1994), a theory ". . . always remains guesswork, and there is no theory that is not beset with problems" (p. 157). As such, treatment specialization can—although not always—encourage people to believe they have found the Truth where little truth exists.

Practitioners using an AMS perspective come to believe that some element of every established practice model, method, or theory may be helpful. Accordingly, every model, method, or theory can be adapted and used in a multi-systemic practice framework. As an AMS practitioner, one neither accepts any single model fully, nor disregards a model entirely if there is potential for helping a client succeed in a way that is compatible with professional social work values and ethics. These practitioners hone their critical thinking skills (Gambrill, 1997, 1990) and apply them in practice, particularly as it pertains to treatment theories, models, and methods. In the context of evidence-based practice (Cournoyer, 2004; Gibbs, 2003), sharpened critical thinking skills allow practitioners to closely read and evaluate practice theories, research, or case reports to recognize the strengths, weakness, and contradictions in theories, models, and/or policy related to social work practice.

Informed Eclecticism

The goal of AMS is for practitioners to develop an approach we call *informed eclecticism*. Informed eclecticism allows the use of multiple methods, interventions, and approaches in the context of practice that: (1) is held together by a perspective or approach that provides consistency, that makes practice choices in a way that makes sense in a particular client's life; and (2) is based, whenever possible, on the latest evidence about its efficacy with particular problems and particular clients. While it is often best to rely on empirical evidence, this data is in its infancy. AMS does not preclude the use of informed practice wisdom and personal creativity in developing intervention plans and approaches. It is up to practitioners to ensure that any treatment based in practice wisdom or that is creatively generated be discussed with colleagues, supervisors, or consultants to ensure theoretical consistency and that it fits within the code of professional ethics.

Informed eclecticism is different from the routine definition of eclecticism—the use of whatever theory, model, or method works best for their clients. While this is the goal of AMS practice specifically and social work practice in general (Timberlake, Farber, & Sabatino, 2004), it is an elusive goal indeed. Informed eclecticism often gets lost in a practitioner's quest to find something that "works." According to Gambrill (1997), eclecticism is "the view that we should adopt whatever theories or methodologies is useful in inquiry, no matter what their source and without worry about their consistency" (p. 93). The most important word in Gambrill's statement is "consistency." While there are practitioners who have managed to develop a consistent, organized, and holistic version of informed eclecticism, this is not the norm.

Too often, uninformed eclecticism resembles the following. A practitioner specializes by modality (individual therapy) and uses a variety of modality-specific ideas and practices in his work with clients; changing ideas and tactics when the approach he normally uses does not "work." This often leaves the practitioner searching (mostly in vain) for the magic intervention—what "works." Moreover, while uninformed eclectic practitioners use interventions from various "schools," they remain primarily wedded to one modality. Hence, they end up confusing themselves and their clients as they search for the "right" approach, rarely looking beyond their chosen modality, and therefore, never actually looking outside of their self-imposed, theoretical cage.

For example, an uninformed eclectic practitioner specializing in individual therapy may try a cognitive approach, a client-centered approach, a Freudian approach, or a behavioral approach. A family therapy specialist may use a structural, strategic, or solution-focused approach. However, in the end, little changes. These practitioners still believe that their clients need individual or family treatment. They rarely consider potentially useful ideas and tactics taken from different modalities that could be used instead of, or in combination with, an individual or family approach, mostly because they base treatment decisions on their chosen modality.

While informed eclecticism is the goal, most find it difficult to find consistency when trying to work from a variety of models at the same time. The informed eclectic practitioners, through experience and empirical evidence, have a unifying approach that serves as the basis for using different models or methods. What is important, according to clinical outcome research, is the consistency of approach in helping facilitate successful client outcome (Gaston, 1990; Miller & Rollnick, 2002; Harper & Lantz, 1996). Trying to be eclectic makes consistency (and treatment success), quite difficult.

What uninformed eclecticism lacks is the framework needed to gain a holistic and comprehensive understanding of the client in the context of his or her life, history, and multiple environments that leads naturally to culturally consistent treatment and intervention decisions. AMS, as it is described here, provides such a framework. It is holistic, integrative, ecological, and based in the latest empirical evidence. It is an inclusive framework that bases treatment decisions on a multi-systemic assessment of specific client history and culture. It is designed, whenever possible, to capitalize on client strengths, be consistent with culturally specific help-seeking behavior, and utilize existing or formulated community-based and/or natural support systems in the client's environment.

Defining Multi-Systemic Client Information

In this section we specifically discuss the different dimensions that comprise AMS practice. This is a general look at what constitutes multi-systemic client life information. There are six levels of information that, when integrated into a life history of clients, demonstrates how multiple theories, models, and approaches can be applied to better understand, assess, and treat clients or client-systems. Generally, the six dimensions (biological, psychological, family, religious/spiritual/existential, social/environmental, and macro) encompass range of information needed to complete a comprehensive, multi-systemic assessment, treatment, and intervention plan with client-systems of all sizes and configurations.

1. Biological Dimension

AMS practitioners need to understand what some have called the "mind-body connection," or the links between social/emotional, behavioral, and potential biological or genetic issues that may be, at least in part, driving the problems presented by clients in practice. As scientific evidence mounts regarding the biological and genetic sources of personal troubles (i.e., some mental illness, etc.), it grows imperative for well-trained AMS practitioners to apply this knowledge in everyday work with clients (Ginsberg, Nackerud, & Larrison, 2004). The responsibility for understanding biology and physical health goes well beyond those working in direct health care practice settings (i.e., hospital, HIV, or hospice practice settings). Issues pertaining to physical health confront practitioners in all practice settings.

For example, practitioners working in mental health settings are confronted daily with issues pertaining to human biology; the sources and determinants of mental illness, differential uses of psychotropic medication, and often, the role played in client behavior by proper nutrition, appropriate health care, and even physical rest. In foster care and/or family preservation, practitioners also confront the effects of parental abuses (i.e., fetal alcohol syndrome [FAS], medication management, and child/adolescent physical and biological development issues).

Beyond learning about the potential biological or physical determinants of various client troubles, having a keen understanding of the potential physical and health risks associated with various behaviors and/or lifestyles places practitioners in the position of intervening to save lives. For example, practitioners working with substance abusing or chemically dependent clients must understand drug pharmacology—especially drug-mixing—to predict potentially life-threatening physical withdrawal effects and/or to prevent intentional or unintentional harm caused by drug overdose (Johnson, 2004).

AMS requires that practitioners keep current with the latest information about human biology, development, genetics, and potential associated health risks facing clients and client-systems in practice. With that knowledge, practitioners can include this information during client assessment, treatment planning, and intervention strategies. It also requires practitioners to know the limits of professional responsibility. That is, social workers are not physicians and should never offer medical advice or guidance that is not supported by properly trained physicians. Therefore, AMS practitioners utilize the appropriate medical professionals as part of assessment, planning, and intervention processes with all clients.

2. Psychological/Emotional Dimension

AMS practitioners need a working knowledge of the ways that psychological and emotional functioning are intertwined with clients' problems and strengths, how issues from this dimension contribute to the way their client or client-system interacts with self and others in their environment, and how their environments influence their psychological and emotional functioning. There are several important skill sets that practitioners must develop to consider issues in this dimension. First, being able to recognize potential problems through a mental screening examination is a skill necessary to all practitioners. Also, having a keen understanding of the *Diagnostic and Statistical Manual of Mental Disorders* (DSM) (American Psychological Association, 2000), including the multi-axial diagnostic process, and recognition of the limits of this tool in the overall multi-systemic assessment process is instrumental. Especially critical is the ability to recognize co-occurring disorders (Johnson, 2004). It is also valuable to learn the Person-in-Environment (PIE) assessment system (Karls & Wandrei, 1994a, 1994b), a diagnostic model developed specifically for social workers to incorporate environmental influences.

In addition to understanding how psychology and emotion affects client mood and behavior, AMS practitioners also know how to employ different theories and models used for treating psychological and emotional functioning problems in the context of a client's multi-systemic assessment and treatment plan. This includes methods of treating individuals, families, and groups. Depending on the client's multi-systemic assessment, each of these modalities or some combination of modalities is appropriate for people with problems in this dimension.

3. Family Dimension

The family is the primary source of socialization, modeling, and nurturing of children. Hence, the family system has a significant impact on people's behavior, and people's behavior has significant impact on the health and well-being of their family system (Johnson, 2004). By integrating a family systems perspective into AMS, practitioners will often be able to make sense of behavior attitudes, beliefs, and values that would otherwise be difficult to understand or explain.

For our purposes, a family is defined as a group of people—regardless of their actual blood or legal relationship—whom clients consider to be members of their family (Johnson, 2004). This definition is designed to privilege clients' perceptions and subjective construction of reality and avoid disagreements over who is or is not in someone's family. So, if a client refers to a neighbor as "Uncle Joe," then that perception represents their reality. What good would it do to argue otherwise? Just as in client engagement discussed earlier, AMS practitioners seek to understand and embrace their client's unique definition of family, rather than imposing a rigid standard that may not fit their perceived reality. This is especially important when dealing with gay and lesbian clients. The law may not recognize gay or lesbian marriage, but AMS practitioners must, if that is the nature of the client's relationship and consistent with their belief system.

It is important to have a working knowledge of different theories and approaches to assessing and treating families and couples, as well as the ability to construct three-generation genograms to help conceptualize family systems and characterize the relationships that exist within the family system and between the family and its environment. Family treatment requires unique skills, specialized post-graduate training, and regular supervision before a practitioner can master the methods and call herself a "family therapist." However, the journey toward mastery is well worth it. Family treatment can be among the most effective and meaningful treatment modalities, often used in conjunction with other modalities (individual and/or group treatment), or as the primary treatment method.

4. Religious/Spiritual/Existential Dimension

Practitioners, students, and social work educators are often wary of exploring issues related to religion and spirituality in practice or the classroom. While there are exceptions, this important dimension often goes unexamined. Exploring people's religious beliefs and/or the tenets of their faith, even if they do not appear to have faith of spiritual beliefs, as they pertain to people's subjective definition of self in relation to the world is an important part of AMS practice.

How clients view themselves in relation to others and their world provides an interesting window into the inner workings of their individual interpretation of culture. The extent that clients have internalized messages (positive, negative, and/or neutral) about their behavior from their faith community or personal spiritual belief systems can lead to an understanding of why people approach their lives and others in the ways they do. Moreover, much can be learned, based on these beliefs, about people's belief in the potential for change, how change occurs, and whom is best suited to help in that change process (if anyone at all), especially as it relates to the many moral and religious messages conveyed about people with problems.

Examination of this dimension goes beyond discovering which church or synagogue clients attend. It is designed to learn how and by what means clients define themselves and their lives in their worlds. What tenets they use to justify their lives, and how these tenets either support their current lives or can be used to help lead them toward change. There is much to be learned about client culture, how people interpret their culture in daily life, and how they view their life in their personal context from an examination of their religious or spiritual beliefs.

Moreover, religious and spiritual belief systems can also be a source of strength and support when considered in treatment plans. For example, while many clients may benefit from attendance at a community support group (i.e., Alcoholics Anonymous, Overeaters Anonymous, etc.) or professional treatment, some will benefit even more from participation in groups and events through local houses of worship. In our experience, many clients unable to succeed in professional treatment or support groups found success through a connection or reconnection with organizations that share their faith, whatever that faith may be.

5. Social/Environmental Dimension

Beyond the individual and family, AMS practitioners look to the client's community, including the physical environment, for important clues to help with engagement, assessment, and intervention planning. People live in communities comprised of three different types: (1) location (neighborhoods, cities, and rural or urban villages), (2) identification (religion, culture, race, etc.), and (3) affiliation (group memberships, subcultures, professional, political/ideological groups, etc.). There are five subdimensions that comprise the social/environmental dimension and incorporate the three types of communities listed above (Johnson, 2004):

1. Local community. This includes learning about physical environment, living conditions, a person's fit within her community, neighborhoods, where and how people live on a daily basis, and how they believe they are treated and/or accepted by community members and the community's power structure (i.e., the police, etc.).

2. Cultural context. This includes learning about clients' larger culture, their individual interpretation of culture, and how it drives or influences their daily life. Also included here is an exploration of histories of oppression and discrimination (individual, family, and community) and a client's subcultural group membership (i.e., drug culture, gang culture, etc.).

3. Social class. Often overlooked by practitioners, "information about people's social class is directly related to information about their families, the goodness-of-fit between the person and environment, and the strengths, resources, and/or barriers in their communities" (Johnson, 2004, p. 226). Some believe that no other demographic factor explains so extensively the differences between people and/or groups (Lipsitz, 1997; Davis & Proctor, 1989). Social class represents a combination of income, education, occupation, prestige, and community. It encompasses how these factors affect people's relative wealth and access to power and opportunity (Johnson, 2004).

4. Social/relational. Human beings are social creatures who define themselves in relation to others (Johnson, 2004). Therefore, it is necessary to know something about people's ability to relate to others in their social environment. This investigation includes loved ones, friends, peers, supervisors, teachers, and others that they relate to in their daily life.

5. Legal history and involvement. Obviously, this subdimension includes information about involvement with the legal system, by the client, family members, and friends and peers. More than recording a simple demographic history, seek to discover their feelings, attitudes, and beliefs about themselves, their place in the world, and how their brushes with the law fit into or influence their worldview.

6. Community resources. Investigate the nature and availability of organizational support, including the role of social service organizations, politics, and your presence as a social worker in a client's life. For example, can clients find a program to serve their needs, or what does seeing a social worker mean within their community or culture? What are the conditions of the schools and the influence of churches, neighborhood associations, and block clubs? More importantly, what is the prevailing culture of the local environment? Are neighbors supportive or afraid of each other, and can a client expect to reside in the present situation and receive the support needed to change?

Be sure to include the professional helping system in this subdimension. Practitioners, their agencies, and the policies that assist or impede the professional helping process join with client-systems as part of the overall system in treatment. In other words, we must consider ourselves as part of the system—we do not stand outside in objective observation. This includes practitioner qualities and styles, agency policies, broader policies related to specific populations, and reimbursement policies, including managed care. All of these factors routinely influence the extent to which clients receive help, how clients are perceived in the helping system and, in the case of reimbursement policies, the method of treatment clients are eligible to receive regardless of how their multi-systemic assessment turns out.

Familiarity with various theories and models of community provide the keys to understanding the role of the social, physical, political, and economic environment in an individual's life. Community models look at the broader environment and its impact on people. Clients or client-systems with issues located in this dimension often respond well to group and family treatment methods. Occasionally, practitioners will be required to intervene at the local neighborhood or community level through organizing efforts and/or personal or political advocacy. For example:

I (Johnson) was treating a client in individual and occasional family treatment when it was discovered that the daughter had been molested by a neighbor. The parents had not reported the molestation. I soon learned that this neighbor was rumored to have molested several young girls in the neighborhood and that nobody was willing to report the molestations. I urged my client to organize a neighborhood meeting of all involved parents at her home. I served as the group facilitator for an intense meeting that ultimately built the community support needed to involve law enforcement. Within days, all of the parents in this group met with law enforcement. The perpetrator was arrested, convicted, and sentenced to life imprisonment.

6. Macro Dimension

AMS practitioners do not stop looking for relevant client information at the local level. They also look for clues in the way that macro issues influence clients, their problems, and potential for change. Knowledge of various laws (local, state, and national) are critical, as well as an understanding of how various social policies are interpreted and enforced in a particular client's life. For example, AMS requires an understanding of how child welfare policies affect the life of a chemically dependent mother, how healthcare policy affects a family's decisions about seeking medical treatment for their children, or how local standards of hygiene or cleanliness affect a family's status and acceptance in their community.

Issues to consider at this level also include public sentiment, stereotypes, and mechanisms of oppression that play a significant role in the lives of people who are not Caucasian, male, middle-class (or more affluent) citizens. Racism, classism, homophobia, and sexism, to name a few, are real threats to people who are attempting to live a "normal" life. An AMS practitioner must understand this reality and learn from clients what their individual perceptions are of these mechanisms and how they affect their problems and potential for change. The macro dimension involves issues such as housing, employment, and public support, along with the dynamics of the criminal justice system. For example, if clients have been arrested for domestic violence, what is the chance they will get fair and just legal representation? If they have been convicted and served jail or prison sentences, what are the chances they will have a reasonable chance of finding sufficient employment upon release?

These issues can be addressed in individual, family, or group treatments. Often, group treatment is an effective way to address issues clients struggle with at the macro level. Group treatment provides clients a way to address these issues in the context of mutual social support and a sense of belonging, helping them realize that they are not alone in their struggles (Yalom, 1995). AMS practitioners also recognize the need for political advocacy and community organizing methods for clients who present with consistent struggles with issues at the macro level.

Summary

The hallmark of AMS is its reliance on and integration of multi-systemic client information into one comprehensive assessment, treatment, and intervention plan. It incorporates knowledge, skills, and values from multiple sources, and relies on various sources of knowledge to paint a holistic picture of people's lives, struggles, strengths and resources, and potentials for change. Practitioners need a current working knowledge of human behavior, social systems theories, the latest social research and practice evaluation results, the impact of public laws and policies, as well as the skills and abilities to plan and implement treatment approaches as needed, in a manner consistent with our definition of informed eclecticism.

Many students new to AMS start out confused because the requirements seem so diverse and complicated. However, as you will see in the case presentations to follow, an organized and efficient practitioner who has learned to think and act multi-systemically can gather large amounts of critically important information about a client in a relatively short period. For this to happen, you must have a deep understanding of various theories, models, and practice approaches that address the various systemic levels considered and be willing to accept that no single model is completely right or wrong. It is always easier to latch on to one model and "go with it." However, the goal of practice is not to be correct or to promote your own ease and comfort, but to develop an assessment and treatment plan that is right for each client, whether or not you would ever use it in your own life. Social work practice is not about the social worker, but the client. It is important never to lose sight of this fact.

Bibliography

American Psychiatric Association (2000). *Diagnostic and statistical manual of mental disorders* (4th ed., TR). Washington, DC: Author.

Appleby, G. A. (2001). Dynamics of oppression and discrimination. In G. A. Appleby, E. Colon, & J. Hamilton (eds.), *Diversity, oppression, and social functioning: Person-in-environment assessment and intervention.* Boston: Allyn and Bacon.

Best, S., & Kellner, D. (1991). *Postmodern theory: Critical interrogations.* New York: Guilford Press.

Cournoyer, B. R. (2004). *The evidence-based social work skills book.* Boston: Allyn and Bacon.

Cox, E. O., & Parsons, R. J. (1994). *Empowerment-oriented social work practice with the elderly.* Pacific Grove, CA: Brooks/Cole.

Davis, L. E., & Proctor, E. K. (1989). *Race, gender, and class: Guidelines for practice with individuals, families, and groups.* Englewood Cliffs, NJ: Prentice-Hall.

Derezotes, D. S. (2000). *Advanced generalist social work practice.* Thousand Oaks, CA: Sage.

Fong, R. (2001). Culturally competent social work practice: Past and present. In R. Fong & S. Furuto (eds.), *Culturally competent practice: Skills, interventions, and evaluations.* Boston: Allyn and Bacon.

Freire, P. (1993). *Pedagogy of the oppressed.* New York: Continuum.

Gambrill, E. (1997). *Social work practice: A critical thinker's guide.* New York: Oxford University Press.

Gambrill, E. (1990). *Critical thinking in clinical practice.* San Francisco: Jossey-Bass.

Gaston, L. (1990). The concept of the alliance and its role in psychotherapy: Theoretical and empirical considerations. *Psychotherapy, 27,* 143–153.

Geertz, C. (1973). *The interpretation of cultures.* New York: Basic Books.

Germain, C. B., & Gitterman, A. (1996). *The life model of social work practice* (2nd ed.). New York: Columbia University Press.

Germain, C. B., & Gitterman, A. (1980). *The ecological model of social work practice.* New York: Columbia University Press.

Gibbs, L. E. (2003). *Evidence-based practice for the helping professions: A practical guide with integrated multimedia.* Pacific Grove, CA: Brooks/Cole.

Ginsberg, L., Nackerud, L., & Larrison, C. R. (2004). *Human biology for social workers: Development, ecology, genetics, and health.* Boston: Allyn and Bacon.

GlenMaye, L. (1998). Empowerment of women. In L. M. Gutierrez, R. J. Parsons, & E. O. Cox (eds.), *Empowerment in social work practice: A sourcebook.* Pacific Grove, CA: Brooks/Cole.

Gordon, J. U. (1993). A culturally specific approach to ethnic minority young adults. In E. M. Freeman (ed.), *Substance abuse treatment: A family systems perspective.* Newbury Park, CA: Sage.

Greif, G. L. (1986). The ecosystems perspective "meets the press." *Social Work, 31,* 225–226.

Harper, K. V., & Lantz, J. (1996). *Cross-cultural practice: Social work practice with diverse populations.* Chicago: Lyceum Books.

Johnson, J. L. (2004). *Fundamentals of substance abuse practice.* Pacific Grove, CA: Brooks/Cole.

Johnson, J. L. (2000). *Crossing borders—Confronting history: Intercultural adjustment in a post-Cold War world.* Lanham, MD: University Press of America.

Karls, J., & Wandrei, K. (1994a). *Person-in-environment system: The PIE classification system for functioning problems.* Washington, DC: NASW.

Karls, J., & Wandrei, K. (1994b). *PIE manual: Person-in-environment system: The PIE classification system for social functioning.* Washington, DC: NASW.

Kozol, J. (1991). *Savage inequalities: Children in America's schools.* New York: Crown Publishers.

Leigh, J. W. (1998). *Communicating for cultural competence.* Boston: Allyn and Bacon.

Lipsitz, G. (1997). Class and class consciousness: Teaching about social class in public universities. In A. Kumar (ed.), *Class issues.* New York: New York University Press.

Longres, J. F. (2000). *Human behavior in the social environment* (3rd ed.). Itasca, IL: F. E. Peacock.

Lum, D. (1999). *Culturally competent practice.* Pacific Grove, CA: Brooks/Cole.

McLaren, P. (1995). *Critical pedagogy and predatory culture: Oppositional politics in a postmodern era.* London: Routledge.

Miley, K. K., O'Melia, M., & DuBois, B. (2004). *Generalist social work practice: An empowerment approach.* Boston: Allyn and Bacon.

Miller, W. R., & Rollnick, S. (2002). *Motivational interviewing: Preparing people to change addictive behavior* (2nd ed.). New York: Guilford Press.

Mills, C. W. (1959). *The sociological imagination.* New York: Oxford University Press.

Parsons, R. J., Gutierrez, L. M., & Cox, E. O. (1998). A model for empowerment practice. In L. M. Gutierrez, R. J. Parsons, & E. O. Cox (eds.), *Empowerment in social work practice: A sourcebook.* Pacific Grove, CA: Brooks/Cole.

Pinderhughes, E. (1989). *Understanding race, ethnicity, and power.* New York: Free Press.

Popper, K. R. (1994). *The myth of the framework: In defense of science and rationality.* Edited by M. A. Notturno. New York: Routledge.

Saleebey, D. (2002). *The strengths perspective in social work practice* (3rd ed.). Boston: Allyn and Bacon.

Smelser, N. J. (1992). Culture: Coherent or incoherent. In R. Munch & N. J. Smelser (eds.), *Theory of culture.* Berkeley, CA: University of California Press.

Timberlake, E. M., Farber, M. Z., & Sabatino, C. A. (2002). *The general method of social work practice: McMahon's generalist perspective* (4th ed.). Boston: Allyn and Bacon.

van Wormer, K., & Davis, D. R. (2003). *Addiction treatment: A strengths perspective.* Pacific Grove, CA: Brooks/Cole.

Yalom, I. (1995). *The theory and practice of group psychotherapy* (4th ed.). New York: Basic Books.

Alice and Eric

Jan Wrenn

The following case involving Alice and her son, Eric, provides an example of the power of grief, loss, and fear in families. By examining their problems and strengths from a multi-systemic, strengths-based approach, I was able to develop an understanding about their presenting problems that allowed for a multi-dimensional intervention plan targeted at their unique needs. This case also demonstrates many of the common issues and dilemmas faced by practitioners in daily practice. I found Alice and Eric interesting as people, and their case became an important part of my ongoing practice education. I hope you find it interesting and instructive too.

Day One—Presenting Information

Eric arrived at the mental health clinic with his Mother, Alice. He was clinging to her and appeared very withdrawn and shy. Alice made little effort to comfort him or encourage any exchange with me. Instead, she made room for him to sit in the burnt orange, overstuffed chair that sat off to the side of my desk. Eric was a cute little boy, with short, light brown hair. He was thinly built (but not too thin) and was normal height for a six-year-old boy. After introductions, I asked Alice to tell me why she and Eric had come to the clinic. She told me that her father died a month earlier and that Eric was having "difficulty" accepting the loss of his grandfather. Alice further explained that she was a single parent, that Eric had no contact with his father, and that his grandfather had filled the roles of father, grandfather, and best friend to Eric. When I asked about how she could tell that Eric was having "difficulty" accepting his grandfather's death, she said, "He's just not himself." I decided to seek a more detailed description of what that meant later.

I asked Alice if she had any previous experience with counseling. She indicated that this was her first experience. As I normally do with new clients, I explained to Alice that I held a masters degree in social work and that I primarily work with families and individuals. I explained that my experience included working with a multitude of problems and complaints and that I have found it important to look at all factors involved in any situation. I also told her that my profession was concerned with helping individuals and families improve their lives, that clients have many resources and strengths to help them reach their goals, and that we would together determine their goals in therapy. I went on to explain what she could expect to happen during our sessions, our various roles in the process, and pertinent agency policies related to confidentiality and informed consent. I also explained to her that my practice was ethically bound to a code of professional ethics (NASW, 2000) and that my job was to ensure that our work abides by the code for her and Eric's protection.

Following the introductory discussion, I attempted to engage Eric by asking him about school, sports, and his favorite television show. These attempts failed. He simply shrugged and continued trying to hide behind Alice. He made no eye contact with me and rarely even looked in my direction. He fidgeted, remained in the chair with his mother (rejecting my offer for him to sit in a separate chair), and asked Alice three times when they could leave. Eric was clearly uncomfortable, or frightened by a stranger asking him questions. Therefore, I returned to Alice for more background information.

Alice wore baggy, ill-fitting clothes; perhaps to cover the approximately 75 extra pounds she carried on her five-foot, eight-inch frame. She had brown hair and wore no makeup. While she was well groomed and clean, either Alice was a woman who did not worry about her appearance, or she did not have time to worry about it. Alice said that Eric's kindergarten teacher had suggested they come to the clinic. Mrs. James, his teacher, called Alice concerned about changes in Eric's behavior. She told Alice that Eric seemed very sad and even tearful at times. Alice said that he had initially been shy in kindergarten, but over the previous two or three months he had become more outgoing and friendly with the other children. That Eric had reverted to his initial behavior in school worried Alice and Mrs. James. Alice also stated that he often cried at home, saying that he missed his grandfather. I asked Eric about this and he nodded in affirmation.

At this point in the session, I wanted to spend a few minutes alone with Alice. I got my opportunity when Eric asked if he could use the bathroom. While Eric was gone, Alice told me that Eric was having nightmares. Because of his nightmares, Eric had been sleeping with her for the previous two weeks. Alice allowed him do so. By the time Eric returned, our first session was about to end. I thanked them for coming, and we arranged for a second session. Much to Eric's delight, they left.

Questions

Before moving on with the case, stop for a few moments and consider the following issues. The author presented information from her initial session with

Alice and Eric, focusing primarily on their presenting problems and her attempts to engage Eric in therapy. The author also foreshadowed issues about working with children, and discussed her initial difficulties of engaging Eric. Given this discussion, and based on the information from this discussion, consider the following questions.

1. What does the professional literature, your experience, and the experience of your student-colleagues state about engaging and treating young children in therapy? Based on your investigation and discussion, what issues should practitioners be aware of in their efforts to develop a therapeutic relationship with child clients?

2. What theoretical models or approaches are discussed in the literature and clinical research evidence that give practitioners the best chance for success with clients presenting similarly to Alice and Eric?

3. If you were the practitioner for this case, what are your initial clinical impressions of Alice and Eric's situation? What appear to be the most significant issues involved in their presenting problems? What larger issues might the information from the first session point towards related to further treatment?

4. Make a list of Alice and Eric's issues and strengths to this point. Further, list what additional information you would need to complete a comprehensive, multi-systemic assessment and clinical diagnostic statement.

Summary of Initial Session

After our first session, I reflected on what I observed in both Alice and Eric. Alice appeared ready for help and eager to get started. I think it will be difficult to build rapport with Eric, given his shy presentation. Unless I can figure out how to reach him, I will have a difficult time figuring out how best to help him. According to Alice, Eric's behaviors included social withdrawal in kindergarten, frequent bouts of crying, and frequent nightmares. I observed that he was clinging to his mother and his unwillingness to communicate in therapy.

According to Carr (2003), children express grief in several ways, including withdrawal from peers, sadness, nightmares, crying, decline in school performance, lack of appetite, and acting younger than one's actual age. In addition, at Eric's age children know that death is irreversible (Carr, 2003). Common among children, many of Eric's symptoms met the criteria for depression (APA, 2000), including sleep disturbances, social withdrawal, sadness, and crying. Since our clinic required a DSM-IV-TR (APA, 2000) diagnosis for all clients by the end of the second session, I focused on this task during the next session. Moreover, according to Piaget's cognitive development theory, children in Eric's age group are concrete thinkers. Thus, any intervention plan would have to be very specific and concrete for him to understand and have a chance for success.

Based on the information gathered during the first session, my initial goals included, build rapport with Alice and Eric, gathering information for assessment and diagnostic purposes, and identifying their strengths, individually and jointly. Although Eric was the identified client, I realized the significance of working with his mother, too. This would help ensure Eric's success in treatment and strengthen their family relationship. I also believed it was important for Alice to deal with her issues so that she could help Eric in her role as his mother.

Client Engagement and History

Early on, my task was to engage Alice and Eric in treatment. I decided to focus initially on Alice so that she could then help me elicit Eric's cooperation. It was also necessary to understand Alice as an individual and mother, to determine what changes she believes would help her family. For the next few sessions, I spent the first part of each session alone with Alice and the second part alone with Eric. I wanted to begin building a relationship with Eric in order to gain his trust. My times alone with Eric provided me the opportunity to understand him better, explore his concerns, help him feel listened to and understood, and assess the impact of his current functions on his overall functioning (Stern, 2002).

Alice

Engaging Alice was easy. She had little social support, including limited contact with her mother and siblings. They lived out-of-state and Alice wanted someone to listen to her and be supportive. This was my job in this case, at least initially. Therefore, I used open-ended questions, making sure to maintain a relaxed but attentive posture along with active listening skills. Alice referred to herself as a "bad" mother because she felt guilty that Eric did not have a father in the household. She "hated" her appearance (answering my questions earlier), her skills and abilities, and her life in general.

Although she had several jobs before Eric was born, she felt incompetent, saying that she couldn't work because of her asthma, high blood pressure, and severe headaches. Each week I asked her about her own grief, her coping strategies, her interests, and her wants and needs. She was able to easily and openly articulate about her life and seemed to find comfort having a venue to share her thoughts and feelings. I purposefully elected not to begin pointing out her strengths until we had established a rapport. This took until the third session. At the end of our session, I mentioned what I saw as her strengths, including her desire to be a good mother, her ability to cope with stressful circumstances, especially after Eric's father left when Eric was two years old, and that she had been a good daughter to her now deceased father. Listening and being supportive were the only tools I needed to establish an excellent therapeutic relationship with her in a relatively short time.

As we talked, Alice began revealing her problems. She reported her difficulties sleeping over the last few months, problems that began before her father died. When asked about her specific sleeping problems, Alice stated that she had difficulty falling asleep and, when she finally did sleep, she frequently woke up and could not go back to sleep. Alice also reported that she felt sad most of the time, and had for several years. However, she reported that her sadness had deepened since her father died. She had lost interest in her usual daily activities, including television and reading to Eric. She reported frequent, daily bouts of crying and believed that she had "low self-esteem."

Alice also stated that she was "very critical of herself," often second-guessing everything she thought, felt, and did on a daily basis. She further stated that she spent "a lot" of time worrying about everything, including Eric, her health, their future, and their personal safety. Alice reported that she also suffered from significant health problems, including asthma and high blood pressure. Her concern with personal safety caused her to stay home most of the time. She reported feeling most safe when she was in her house. At this point, I began wondering about Alice's potential for suicide. Hence, I asked her if she ever thought about killing herself. While she stated that she had thought about it at different times in her life, she was not currently thinking about it. I let her know emphatically that she could discuss these thoughts and feelings with me at any time.

Family-of-Origin

Her family-of-origin was troubled when she was young. Alice recalled that her mother divorced her father when she was ten years old. Her father never revealed, even later in life, the reasons behind their divorce. After her mother left, she and her father grew extremely close. Because her father never spoke about it, Alice never understood why her mother left the family. She said that this event had left a "scar" on her life. Since that time, Alice had distrusted most people, afraid that they would leave unannounced. Hence, she had very few friends in school, had not kept in touch with them over the years, and had developed few adult friendships as well. Alice and her father attended church together regularly. This stopped in the last few months because of her father's illness. She said that she missed this weekly event. Alice's father had become her primary social support system, and his death left her lacking friends and supportive relationships where she could talk about her life and problems. She was alone as a parent and adult woman.

Alice and Eric lived in a small house owned by her father. She had not worked since Eric was born. After her husband left her four years earlier, Alice and Eric were on public assistance. Her father helped her financially when she needed it. Alice was intimidated by the prospect of having to work again, mainly because of her low self-esteem and symptoms of depression that began well before her father died.

Alice was reticent about the circumstances of her divorce. She classified this as one more example of people leaving her alone. Eric had little contact with his father since the divorce. His grandfather had taken over the role of father during his short life. Alice said that she had not dated since her divorce, and had no interest in "finding a man" at this point in her life. Given her beliefs about the nature of relationships, this did not surprise me at all.

Eric

Engaging Eric was not easy. His shyness presented a significant barrier to the process. Luckily, Alice helped convince Eric to spend time alone with me. She comforted him by saying that she would be in the waiting room if he needed her. The first two weeks, I spent time playing checkers with Eric, a game that he loved playing with his grandfather. Although I was able to engage him in checkers, he remained shy and nontalkative. We also played other board games. Gradually, Eric grew comfortable being alone with me. After a few weeks, I introduced a therapeutic game, called Ungame. The Ungame asks players to answer questions about their life, using real or imagined situations. It allows the practitioner to gain insight into the client's thoughts, fears, beliefs, dreams, and goals in a safe environment.

After a couple of weeks of playing this game, we began taking walks outside and talking about what we saw in the environment. One day he mentioned his grandfather, which allowed us to begin talking about the things they did together. I was careful not to push him with specific questions, instead asking him to tell me about times he shared with his grandfather. My goal was to keep our time together as nonconfrontational and nonthreatening as possible until I was confident that he was willing to disclose more in-depth information. I wanted to create an environment where Eric felt safe with me. Early on, I interpreted his willingness to return each week as evidence that we were developing a trusting relationship.

In addition to the presenting problems offered by Alice during the first session, Eric also presented additional symptoms and behaviors that needed attention. First, Eric missed his grandfather "a lot." They were especially close, and grandfather was Eric's primary male figure. Since his grandfather died, Eric had been having trouble falling asleep and, when he did sleep, experienced bad dreams and nightmares about his grandfather. Additionally, it seems that loss, or at least the potential for significant loss, had become a central theme for Eric. For example, through our conversation and during conversation with Alice, I learned that since grandfather's death, Eric did not want to leave his mother, and said that he "worries" about her all the time. He was also having nightmares about his mother leaving or dying. Alice also reported that Eric has taken to crying several times per day, and she says that he seems to be sad.

As stated earlier, Eric's kindergarten teacher reported similar behaviors. She said that Eric had ceased his usual interactions with friends and was sad most of the time. Eric said that he did not like his friends at school anymore, and would rather be at home with his mother. The interpersonal gains he had made since beginning school had disappeared. Eric now appeared to be a very sad, shy, and withdrawn six-year-old boy who did not want to attend school or interact with anyone but his mother.

Multi-Systemic Assessment Information

I was happy with our first two sessions. I had gathered important information about Alice and Eric. However, I knew that I had to continue engaging them so that I could gather enough information for an accurate final assessment, treatment, and intervention plan. Although I had begun to identify their strengths, I would continue using a strengths-based approach throughout the treatment process. The strengths perspective is an important part of social work practice. It provides a framework for focusing on client problems and strengths simultaneously. The strengths perspective believes that everyone has inherent strengths and resources for self-help, regardless of how difficult his or her lives and problems may seem. The strengths perspective contributes to better client engagement by promoting collaboration. It also serves as a constant reminder to practitioners about people's growth and change capabilities (Cooper & Lesser, 2002).

Client assessment is both a process and a product. That is, accurate assessment is ongoing throughout treatment and requires successful client engagement. In the end, client assessment becomes a working and changing document that is the centerpiece of a treatment planning and intervention process. Assessments are not static, client lives always change in ways that affect treatment goals and intervention choices (Johnson, 2004).

As part of the assessment process, I regularly ask and answer several questions of myself as I prepare to work with different clients. I discuss the relevant questions and answers for this case below.

1. What assumptions was I making about this family?   I assumed that this family wanted to change, that they had the ability to change, and that they had strengths and resources to affect change.

2. How was I interpreting information about this family?   I needed more information about their interactions with their environment, about their family functioning (roles, communication, traditions, beliefs, problem-solving abilities, etc.), as well as individual and family strengths and resources.

3. What other information did I need and what tools could I use to gather this information?   I decided to use a genogram and an eco-map as assessment tools. A genogram would show Alice's family relationships in a detailed way, which I hoped would reveal significant factors about her history. An eco-map would indicate how the family interacted with outside systems and provide a basis for exploring information about their environment. The social work profession's emphasis on person-in-environment (PIE) is important because people often must change in relation to external systems to improve their lives.

4. Did I need collateral information? If so, from whom?   After I had obtained permission by asking Alice to sign a release of information form, I talked with Eric's kindergarten teacher. I wanted her to discuss any behavior changes in Eric since his grandfather's death.

Questions

Now that the author has presented more information about Alice and Eric, and before reading her clinical assessment and diagnoses below, you perform this exercise based on your education, experience, the professional literature, and best practices evidence. To increase the learning potential of this exercise, you may want to do this in a small group with other students in your course.

1. The author discussed using a genogram and eco-map to help with her assessment. We did not include her version so that you would not be influenced by her ideas. Therefore, based on the information contained above, construct a three-generation genogram and eco-map that represent Alice and Eric's personal, familial, and environmental circumstances. What further information do you need to complete this exercise? What patterns do these two important graphical assessment tools demonstrate?

2. Building on the list you began earlier, complete a list of their issues and strengths.

3. Write a two- to three-page narrative assessment that encompasses Alice and Eric's multi-systemic issues and strengths. Review Chapter 1 if needed. This narrative should provide a comprehensive and multi-systemic explanation of their life as they prepare to undergo therapy with the author.

4. Try to identify the theoretical model or approach that you use to guide your assessment. According to the literature, what other theoretical options are available and how would these change the nature of your assessment?

5. End by developing multi-axial DSM-IV-TR diagnoses for both Alice and Eric. Be sure to look for evidence of multiple diagnoses on Axis I. Provide the list of client symptoms that you used to justify your diagnostic decisions. What, if any, information was missing that would make this an easier task?

Cultural Competence

Practitioners must understand their own values and beliefs and have the self-awareness to monitor how their own thinking affects their work with clients. Additionally, it is vital that social workers respect all clients as unique individuals, entitled to having their own values and beliefs. We must also abide by the NASW Code of Ethics (NASW, 2000) that value clients as individuals, free to make their own choices about treatment. Although I have worked with many single-parent families, I could not assume that Alice and Eric were similar to the others. Although many single-parent families might have similar issues or concerns, they should never be stereotyped or categorized. Each family system is unique, and my job was to learn how this particular family approached the world and their issues. At every point in our professional relationship, I was careful to think of them as unique individuals in a unique family. I accomplished this by continually asking for more information to guard against making assumptions based on my experiences with other families or my personal assumptions about how families are supposed to be or people "should" grieve the loss of loved ones.

My Ethical Dilemma

While working with Alice and Eric, my primary ethical dilemma involved my lack of training and experience with children. I had little practice experience with children, had never performed play therapy, had no play therapy training, and no experience or training in working with children's grief and loss. I lacked confidence that I could handle this case successfully and was reluctant to continue with them after the first session. I consulted with my supervisor, who said that there were no other therapists to take the case, so I had to do the work. I was told to learn some things "on my own" about how to handle this case, and to do my best for them.

I immediately purchased books on children's grief and loss, several children's books about grief and loss, and on play therapy. After reading these books, I felt even more intimidated. The NASW Code of Ethics states that clients have a right to competent practice. I seriously questioned whether I could provide the level of competence they needed. However, there were no other options, and these people wanted and needed help. I decided to do the best I could and seek professional help when I needed it. In addition to weekly supervision meetings, I regularly presented at our weekly case conference for feedback and support from others with experience in this area. With these supports in place, my confidence grew. I also talked with colleagues about the case individually. As the weeks passed, my confidence increased, as did my ability to handle the case.

Questions

We credit the author for her willingness to share her lack of training and experience with children, and the dilemma she faced as a result. Our experience suggests that this is often the case in practice. In fact, most practitioners are unprepared when they begin working with clients, or when clients present new constellations of symptoms or from demographic groups we are unfamiliar with over the course of our careers. There is no way to prepare for every practice eventuality or client presentations. Yet, others believe differently. These people believe that practitioners should never work with clients or client problems without previous education, training, or experience in a particular area or with a particular population. Yet, in real, daily practice, most do not have this luxury.

1. In the context of the discussion above, go to the professional literature, including literature on practice ethics, and explore what others in the helping professions believe about this issue. Looking at all sides of the argument, what

position do you take on this issue? Should the author have continued with the case, or removed herself?

2. If and when you find yourself in this position, what approach would you take? If you decided to remain with the case as the author did, what course of action would you take, in addition to the author's plan, to prepare yourself to work with your new client?

3. The author's supervisor made her stay with the case because there was nobody else at the clinic with the time to take on Alice and Eric. Explore this for a moment. This, too, commonly occurs in practice. To develop your position on this issue, continue exploring the practice literature and code of ethics as a way to contextualize and defend your position.

Multi-Systemic Assessment: Alice

After several sessions with Alice and based on the information discussed earlier, I summarized her history and presenting concerns as:

1. History of depression
2. History of anxiety
3. Multiple loss issues (mother leaving when she was ten, husband, father)
4. Significant health problems
5. Concern about Eric and about her parenting abilities
6. Low self-esteem

Alice indicated that her main goal in therapy was to learn how to help Eric. That is, she wanted to learn to become a "better mother." She also indicated that she wanted to learn how to accept personal loss. I believed that her personal losses, depression, anxiety, and low self-esteem were related and that relief in one area would have a positive affect on the others.

I used formal and informal tools during the assessment. Formally, I asked Alice to complete the Beck Depression Inventory, a well-known tool available in the public domain (Beck et al., 1961). This standardized test provides a baseline measure of depression, helping to determine whether Alice's depression eased over the course of treatment. Additionally, I constructed an eco-map and genogram. Informally, I used observation and questioning, as well as client self-reports. I asked her to keep track of how often she felt sad and anxious. We used this information as a baseline, hoping that the number of times each day she felt sad and anxious would decrease during treatment.

I also decided to refer her to our psychiatrist for an evaluation. I recommended that the psychiatrist consider antidepressant medication for Alice because of her presenting symptoms of depression (APA, 2000). My role as her therapist was to determine whether the severity of her symptoms warranted a psychiatric referral and recommendation for medication. I determined that Alice might benefit from such a referral, because Alice had trouble sleeping, little appetite, was sad and cried often, had low self-esteem, a history of suicidal thoughts, and her role as mother was compromised because of her symptoms of depression.

A social worker's role and responsibility pertaining to client medication include determining relevant symptoms, assessing the severity of the symptoms, referring clients to a psychiatrist, monitoring client progress, and explaining client medication questions, especially related to potential side effects. Practitioners working in mental health must be willing to find the relevant facts about medication and be willing to discuss these issues whenever clients have concerns. This will help clients comply with their medical regimen.

Multi-Systemic Assessment: Eric

During our sessions, I determined that Eric did not have learning disabilities or health problems. He was average weight and height for his age. Alice told me that Eric did not have any significant difficulties as an infant, toddler, or in early childhood. He routinely met normal childhood milestones, such as talking and walking, at the appropriate developmental age.

Alice claimed that Eric enjoyed "typical things" such as reading, watching television, playing games, sports, and fishing. Eric had mainly shared the latter two activities with his grandfather. She said that Eric and she spent most of their evenings at home and had little interaction with other people. Since his grandfather died, Eric had demonstrated no interest in his usual activities. According to Alice, his grandfather "meant the world" to Eric. She said they were together everyday and that Eric loved spending time with him. They watched television, played checkers and other games, went fishing, and watched local baseball games. She said that Eric never needed disciplinary attention because he was always obedient.

I also learned from Alice that Eric dreamt about both his grandfather and his mother dying. Alice tried to reassure him that she was fine, to no avail. In reality, Alice was overweight, had high blood pressure, asthma, and did not take good care of her health. It made sense to me that Eric would worry about his mother dying, since she was now the only person in the world with whom he had a close connection. Further, Alice said that on the mornings after his death dreams, Eric did not want to go to school. On some occasions, Alice allowed Eric to stay home.

Mrs. James, Eric's kindergarten teacher, described Eric as appropriate, engaging, and responsive when directly questioned. She said he was normally interactive with other children, polite, cooperative, and alert. However, since his grandfather's death, Mrs. James had become concerned about Eric's mental status because he had become withdrawn, sad, and tearful in school.

After collecting this information, I determined that Eric met the criteria for DSM-IV-TR (APA, 2000) diagnoses: Major Depressive episode (based on withdrawal, sadness, crying, sleep problems), Separation Anxiety (based on his clinging to his mother and not wanting to leave), and Grief. Because he was a child, I knew the importance of Eric's age and developmental level in assessment and treatment planning. At Eric's age, he should have the capacity to think in concrete, logical terms. I also knew that children from two to four years old typically experience separation anxiety. However, children who experience loss and trauma sometimes regress to earlier developmental stages. I concluded that this was the case with Eric, primarily because of the loss of his grandfather.

Multi-systemically, Alice and Eric were isolated from external systems. Alice did not socialize, and Eric only socialized at school. Neither Alice no Eric had friends or other relationships for support. Over the years, this family remained self-contained, with the only external relationship being with Eric's school, church, and the State Welfare office. Hence, this family lacked community resources. This issue would have to be addressed in therapy if changes were to occur and maintain after therapy ended.

Diagnostic Summary

After careful consideration of their information, symptoms, problems, and strengths, I recommended the following multi-axial (APA, 2000) diagnoses for Alice and Eric.

Alice
Axis I	Dysthymic Disorder
Axis II	No diagnosis
Axis III	High Blood Pressure, Asthma, Headaches
Axis IV	Lack of support, Grief
Axis V	60 (GAF current)

Eric
Axis I	Depression
	Separation Anxiety
Axis II	No diagnosis
Axis III	None
Axis IV	Lack of support, Grief
Axis V	55 (GAF current)

Questions

Before moving on, compare the assessment and diagnostic statement you developed earlier to the author's. Where do you find points of agreement and disagreement? Discuss these issues with student-colleagues and use the professional literature to analyze the differences.

1. What implications for treatment arise, because of differences in assessment and diagnoses?

2. Explain these differences as part of a treatment plan. That is, develop a treatment plan for Alice and Eric from your assessment. Include types of treatment, the theoretical model, or approach (approaches) you would use, and how these differ from those used by the author.

Treatment and Intervention Planning

Based on the assessment and diagnoses discussed above, we first needed to formulate treatment goals before proceeding to intervention. I asked Alice to determine her goals for Eric and herself. She said that her primary concern was Eric. She worried about his sadness and nightmares. She also said that she needed to become a "better mother." I asked her if she wanted to resolve her issues with grief and loss. She agreed. We also agreed on other goals, including decreasing her symptoms of anxiety and depression and increasing her self-esteem.

I asked Eric if he wanted help with anything. He stated that he wanted me to help him "not to feel so sad." I also asked him if we could talk about him getting to know other people. He said, "That would be OK." Eric, Alice, and I also discussed his depression and agreed that we should try to decrease his symptoms significantly.

Treatment Plan: Alice

To help Alice meet her treatment goals, I decided to select interventions from several theoretical frameworks. Interventions based on Murray Bowen's intergenerational approach would help Alice understand the impact of her family-of-origin on her current functioning. In looking at her genogram, Alice was able to recognize family dynamics that were a painful part of her history. I also used a family systems approach to provide information about the connectedness of her family's subsystems (Alice and her father; her father and Eric; and Alice and Eric) and how external systems (neighbors, Eric's kindergarten, former church) affected their family.

I used techniques from a solution-focused model to focus Alice on finding solutions based on her strengths. That is, I want her to employ solutions to problems that had already worked in the past. I used scaling questions to help assess treatment progress or regression. Finally, I used a cognitive-behavioral approach to deal with Alice's low self-esteem, depression, and anxiety. This approach targets distorted thinking patterns that lead to counterproductive thoughts, beliefs, and actions. Recurrent thought patterns, sometimes referred to as irrational beliefs, contribute to people's feels, thoughts, and actions. Helping Alice identify her irrational thoughts and to replace them with more realistic, positive thoughts could significantly affect her low self-esteem, depression, and anxiety.

Hence, we operationalized Alice's goals into the following intervention plan, complete with indicators of progress and/or regression toward goal achievement.

Goal 1: *Accept loss of father*

Objectives:
a. Journal thoughts and memories of father as they occur
b. Write a letter to mother and siblings expressing her grief and memories
c. Read a book on coping with a loss

Goal 2: *Demonstrate ability to function independently*

Objectives:
a. Make two important decisions and feel confident about them
b. Develop three personal goals and work to achieve them

Goal 3: *Implement behaviors to promote independence for Eric*

Objectives:
a. Enroll Eric in at least one social activity with peers
b. Permit and encourage Eric to socialize with his friends at their home

Goal 4: *Increase self-esteem (Improve baseline self-report score of "two" on a scale of 1–10, with 10 being highest, to at least a "six or seven.")*

Objectives:
a. Replace negative self-talk with positive affirmations
b. Increase self-awareness by journaling and reflecting on thoughts and behaviors
c. Develop a hobby or other pleasurable activity to engage in regularly

Goal 5: *Decrease symptoms of depression and anxiety (ability to sleep through the night), increased energy level, and decrease frequency of crying; decrease feelings of being "overwhelmed" and of not wanting to leave her home*

Objectives:
a. Take standardized tests to assess levels of anxiety and depression
b. Engage in some aerobic exercise at least three times per week
c. Use cognitive behavioral strategies (self-talk) to help relieve anxiety

Strategies:
1. Cognitive Therapy—increase self-esteem; reduce anxiety
2. Cognitive-Behavioral—function independently; relieve symptoms of depression
3. Solution-focused therapy—increase self-esteem (scaling)
4. Family Systems Theory—grief and loss issues related to death of father

5. Bowen's Intergenerational Theory—family of origin losses
6. Referral for psychiatric evaluation to determine the need for anti-anxiety and/or antidepressant medication
7. Individual sessions weekly; to be evaluated in three months
8. Family therapy with Eric two times per month for three months
9. Evaluation three weeks before projected termination date to determine whether termination can occur or if treatment should continue

Questions

1. Compare the treatment plan you established earlier with the author's treatment plan. What differences and similarities exist between the plans? How do you account for the differences? Use the professional literature and practice evidence to analyze both plans and the differences between them.

2. Develop a revised treatment plan from information provided by the author, your original plan, and the practice literature. What does the evidenced-based practice literature say are the most effective ways to treat clients with Alice and Eric's problems and strengths? Using the rationale from the literature and your experience, develop a position on this issue.

Course of Treatment: Alice

Early on in treatment, Alice and I agreed that before she could make progress on other goals, she needed to begin "feeling better" emotionally. Hence, I referred her to our psychiatrist immediately; she was prescribed medication to treat her depression. The doctor told her to expect changes in her symptoms in approximately three weeks. For the next two weeks, Alice talked about her grief and loss and her family-of-origin, especially her mother and siblings. Alice was angry that her mother abandoned the family. She stated that she had "no desire to feel differently." By the third week of treatment, Alice began benefiting from the medication. She reported a significant change in mood, "more energy," was crying less, and sleeping better. Alice was amazed by how good it felt to sleep for several hours without waking.

Once her symptoms receded, I asked her if she was willing to write about her feelings in a personal journal. I also asked her to read a book I provided about losing a parent. Now that she felt better, Alice was eager to continue her progress and agreed. We spent time during several sessions talking about the grief process, typical reactions, and the recovery process. I have found that journaling is an effective intervention for clients struggling with grief and loss. It provides them a private place to explore feelings and thoughts that they often bottle up. It also allows clients overwhelmed with worries and fears, to "place" them into a journal at a specific time each day, allowing many people relief from constant and overwhelming symptoms. Once they understand that they can deal with their thoughts and fears "later," they no longer feel overwhelmed by them all day, every day. I explained to Alice that she should journal once per day about her feelings and thoughts, particularly about her father. I said that she could share any portion of her journal with me that she wanted, but only if she wanted to share. I emphasized that the journal was her personal record of her feelings and thoughts, and that she had the right to keep it private. After a period of journaling, Alice said that writing about her father was helpful. She began bringing her journal to therapy each week to share portions with me.

After a few weeks, I initiated a series of behavioral interventions with Alice. For example, since her doctor gave permission, I asked Alice to exercise one day per week between sessions. We agreed that she would perform any exercise she wanted for at least 20 minutes. She chose to walk for 30 minutes. After her success with exercise, Alice agreed to walk three days per week. Alice benefited from renewed physical activity. She saw walking as a way to reduce weight, relieve stress, and improve her sometimes failing health concerns.

I also began using cognitive restructuring techniques. I asked Alice to record her "self-talk" for one week along with her feelings of anxiety. I further asked her to note what was happening just prior to negative self-talk and anxious feelings. The following week, we discussed how she could substitute positive "self-talk." I asked her to practice this technique aloud during our session. Soon, Alice was practicing her new techniques at home, between sessions. At this point, all seemed to be progressing well, and I was pleased with her remarkable progress.

Problems Resurfaced

Commonly, clients do not continue their remarkable progress consistently throughout therapy. As I like to say, change is often a matter of taking "two steps forward, and one step backwards." This happened to Alice. After a remarkable string of successes, during the next session Alice reported feeling discouraged. She said that she had been unable to work on her thinking patterns because she began feeling "sad" again. She reported additional setbacks, too. Alice stated that her symptoms of depression had increased and that she was feeling "worthless." Fearing the worst, I again explored the possibility of suicidal thinking. She stated that she had thought about it, but had no concrete plans or lethal means. This suggested to me that she was not significantly at-risk for suicide at this time. I asked how she was able to overcome her suicidal thoughts. Alice stated that she kept focusing on how bad her death would be for Eric. She was motivated to live, always a good thing with depressed clients.

Given this turn of events, my ethical responsibility required that I take every step possible to ensure her safety. I considered what to do if she became suicidal again. That is, should I request hospitalization or proceed on a less intensive basis? I also had to consider her lack of social support in times of crisis (whom could Alice turn to if her suicidal thoughts returned and I was unavailable?). Since Alice did not have a well-formed suicide plan, I asked her to agree to a suicide contract. A suicide contract is often used in these circumstances. In this written contract, both the client and practitioner agree to take certain actions in the event that the client becomes suicidal in the future. I agreed to provide Alice with places to call in the event she became suicidal, and Alice agreed to contact our clinic's suicide hot-line in the event that her suicide thoughts returned.

Given the downturn in her coping skills, I considered referring her for medication review and a possible change in her prescription. I referred her back to our psychiatrist, who was able to see her two days later. The psychiatrist increased the dosage of her antidepressant medication, believing that this would provide Alice with symptom relief in two weeks or so.

Back on Track

Over the next two sessions, Alice made little progress. However, she finally began improving during the third week following her downturn. Three weeks before our initial planned termination date, we assessed her progress. She was again feeling more positive and eager to work on her goals. She no longer had suicidal thoughts, was sleeping better, feeling more energy, and crying less. Our goal review helped to measure her progress to date and, in this instance, renegotiate her treatment goals. Alice reluctantly agreed to attend a grief and loss support group. She had not read the book I had suggested, claiming that the reading was "too hard." However, she did report overall improvement and attributed it mostly to journal writing. She claimed that her experience of grief was less intense. She was able to talk about her dad without crying. She was exercising two or three times per week, and had begun attending a support group for single parents. This was a major step toward her goal of increasing social support.

Additionally, Alice reported her self-esteem at a "four" on a scale of 1–10. We also noted success with parenting. Alice had enrolled Eric in Little League baseball, encouraged him to have friends over to the house, and allowed him to visit a friend's home. Alice said that her depression had not disappeared. She continued to have problems sleeping through the night. Her new goal was to increase her self-reported self-esteem from "four" to at least a "six or seven." While she was definitely improving, I was pleased to hear that Alice wanted more.

While neither Alice nor I believed that she was ready to terminate therapy, I was pleased with her progress and believed that she was doing well, considering her earlier setback. Once her medication was adjusted, her mood changed, allowing her to work on issues other than her depression and anxiety. I was encouraged that she had no recurrence of suicidal thoughts since her medication was increased. After this review, we renegotiated a new termination date for three months hence. We also renegotiated Alice's treatment goals to include a target of six or seven on her self-esteem scale, decrease depression and anxiety symptoms through cognitive restructuring, and continue to work on her experience of grief and loss, and her intense feelings toward her mother and siblings.

Maintaining Progress

During the next three months, Alice remained committed to her new goals and made progress toward achieving each. She became increasingly aware of how her thoughts affected her feelings and behaviors, and gained significant control over her self-talk. Journaling again proved an effective tool to help with her experience of grief and loss. She saw herself as a better mother for Eric, claiming that they had begun exploring interests and relationships independent of each other. Alice developed friendships with two women from her grief support group, and another woman from her single-parent support group. She happily reported that she was better able to be Eric's parent and to allow him to be a child. We attribute these changes as leading to her self-reported changes in self-esteem. After three months of therapy, Alice happily reported that her self-esteem had reached a "six" on her scale. She was also better able to manage her symptoms of depression and anxiety with a combination of a reduced dosage of medication, self-talk, and regular physical exercise. Alice retook the Beck Depression Inventory. It clearly demonstrated that her symptoms had subsided.

The most difficult issue for Alice continued to be writing a letter to her mother and siblings to claim her anger and hurt at their having left the family many years earlier. However, she finally relented. Once she wrote and mailed the letter, Alice reported a significant reduction in her experience of grief and loss. Given the positive review of her progress, we decided that Alice was ready for termination, three weeks hence. I discuss her termination later.

Questions

1. Take a moment to review Alice's progress in treatment. Based on the author's description, the professional literature, and the latest practice evidence, what occurred to account for her progress?

2. What was the theoretical approach or combination of approaches that appeared to work best for Alice?

3. Based on the work you have done earlier, what additional intervention(s) would you recommend for Alice? Use the literature and latest evidence to justify your recommendations.

Treatment Plan: Eric

Because of his age, I needed to think differently about Eric's treatment plan. From my reading and consultation with more experienced therapists, I concluded that play therapy and behavioral therapy were most appropriate. Play therapy offers children the opportunity to express emotions in a safe way, along with providing a safe vehicle for children to identify and express the feelings related to the current experiences (Stern, 2002). Behavioral therapy makes use of positive reinforcement by rewarding positive behavior. I wanted to reinforce Eric's attending kindergarten rather than staying home with his mother. I asked Alice to use a sticker chart to record school attendance.

Goal 1: Accept loss of grandfather

Objectives:
a. Express his grief in age appropriate ways through reading children's books on grief, drawings, paintings, and activity workbooks
b. Express his anxiety, fear, and anger in appropriate ways

Goal 2: Increase social interactions with others/Decrease symptoms of separation anxiety

Objectives:
a. Become involved in one weekly social activity
b. Visit friends in their homes and have them to his home
c. Mother will use sticker chart and give a sticker for school attendance

Goal 3: Decrease symptoms of depression (sadness, crying, withdrawal, decreased appetite, sleep difficulties)

Objectives:
a. Express his feelings in an appropriate way

Goal 4: Decrease family's level of dependence

Objectives:
a. Spend time apart in activities with other people
b. Enroll Eric in "Big Brother" program

Strategies:
1. Behavioral Therapy
2. Play Therapy
3. Individual sessions weekly for three months
4. Family sessions two times per month for three months
5. Evaluate two to three weeks prior to the planned last session to determine whether to plan termination or to continue treatment.

Questions

1. Compare the treatment plan you established above with the author's treatment plan. What differences and similarities exist between the plans? How do you account for the differences? Use the professional literature and practice evidence to analyze both plans, and the differences between them.

2. Develop a revised treatment plan from information provided by the author, your original plan, and the practice literature. What does the evidenced-based practice literature say are the most effective ways to treat clients with Eric's problems and strengths? Using the rationale from the literature and your experience, develop a position on this issue.

Course of Treatment: Eric

The strengths perspective claims that practitioners should focus on strengths during assessment and treatment planning. Using a strengths perspective provides the structure for building self-confidence that stimulates hope (Cowger, 1994). During my first session with Eric, I began focusing on his strengths. For example, I noticed his eagerness to please his mother, his desire to learn in kindergarten (his mother told me he loved learning to read and write and had always enjoyed having books read to him), and his personality (his mother described him as helpful, kind, and cheerful). In subsequent weeks, I identified other strengths, including his patience, social skills (he was polite and engaging, after getting over his initial shyness), and his resilience. Affirming resilience can empower young clients (Vernon, 2004). I accomplished this by emphasizing Eric's desire to attend kindergarten, his desire to remember and honor his grandfather, and his helpfulness at home, despite his struggles with grief and depression.

After the slow start to engagement described earlier, I believed we had sufficiently joined so that we could begin to initiate interventions that targeted his symptoms and difficulties. To help him accept the loss of his grandfather and appropriately express his emotions, I began reading him stories about children who had lost loved ones. He seemed to like this approach. Therefore, during each subsequent session after small talk about his week, kindergarten activities, and so on, I read him a children's book on grief. After the story was finished, Eric and I would discuss it. I also used an activity workbook in which he drew various pictures of his grandfather and himself. In several sessions, he drew pictures of himself that reflected his environment, his interactions with others, and his mood.

I asked Eric to play with the various puppets, stuffed animals, small plastic people, animals, houses, and cars while I observed, asked questions about his activities, and commented on his actions. In play, I observed themes of sadness, fear, and anger. Each week, I asked him to choose from various faces demonstrating a range of emotions the face that best described him that day. There was a dramatic change over the course of therapy. He went from choosing sad faces initially to happy faces later in our relationship. He also drew and colored pictures showing what he and his mom were doing at his house. In these pictures, the themes changed over time from little activity and interaction to creative and enjoyable activities.

Eric and his mother adopted a puppy. Subsequently, his pictures focused on his play with the dog. Eric said that he enjoyed taking care of his puppy. His mood had begun to change dramatically. As therapy progressed, Eric continued to experience decreased symptoms of depression. He stopped having nightmares about his grandfather or his mother. His sleep patterns were better, his social withdrawal disappeared, and his sadness dissipated.

To deal further with the loss of his grandfather, I asked Eric to bring photos of them together. We spent a lot of time looking at these photographs while Eric told me what each represented to him. With my encouragement, he put together a photo album of his grandfather, and a scrapbook of drawings of things they did together, along with other meaningful mementos. These activities helped Eric accept the loss of his grandfather by preserving his memories in a tangible way. Eric made the decision to continue attending baseball games, play baseball, and remember his grandfather's love of the game.

Family Sessions

As part of Eric's treatment, we met in family therapy two times per month over the course of the six months I treated Alice. As a family, we focused on decreasing their level of dependence on each other. Each week I assigned a homework assignment for the family. The assignments initially related to shared memories of Alice's father. I asked them to bring pictures and/or other reminders of the things the three of them enjoyed together. I then asked them to think of things they could do together to honor the memory of the father/grandfather. They each chose pictures to frame and hang in a special place in their living room.

Both Alice and Eric talked about how much Eric's grandfather enjoyed reading. I asked them to think about something that they could do to make him proud of them. They said he liked helping people by working weekly at a soup kitchen, volunteering at the hospital, and helping neighbors. They decided to volunteer at the soup kitchen on a regular basis in his honor. Additionally, they began growing more independent, each having a small social circle and various interests apart from each other.

Progress Maintained

As the end of our three-month agreement approached, Eric's separation anxiety had significantly decreased. During our work together, Alice had encouraged him to interact more with friends. Eric began to enjoy his friends again, as he had prior to his grandfather's death. He was active with Little League practice and games. His mother regularly attended his games, and Eric looked forward to seeing her in a certain spot in the stands. His dog also occupied Eric's time and attention. I asked Alice if she would consider requesting a Big Brother for Eric at a local agency; she agreed. The agency linked Eric with an eighteen-year-old. They began immediate and regular contact almost immediately. This intervention was designed to further enhance Eric's independence from his mother, increase his support system, and offer another person with whom he could share, similarly to how he shared with his grandfather.

Given my initial hesitance at working with Eric, I was pleased with his progress. The most important lesson I learned during the process was that children cannot be reached in the same way as adults, that progress needs to be at the child's pace, that patience is critical, and that I, as the therapist, must be flexible and adaptable in treatment. I was amazed at Eric's strength and his ease in adapting to changes in his life. I am convinced, however, that we would have had less success if I had not been working simultaneously with Alice. She was largely responsible for initial engagement, and her cooperation throughout the process was stellar.

Questions

1. Take a moment to review Eric's progress in treatment. Based on the author's description, the professional literature, and the latest practice evidence, what occurred to account for her progress?

2. What was the theoretical approach or combination of approaches that appeared to work best for Eric?

3. Based on the work you have done earlier, what additional intervention(s) would you recommend for Eric? Use the literature and latest evidence to justify your recommendations.

Termination/Outcome/Follow-Up

Once we decided to terminate, Alice agreed to review her progress by reading portions of her journal that she believed were most reflective of her growth in therapy. When she finished reading her highly personal account of her life, I commended Alice on her successes and her strengths as an individual and as a mother.

Eric had changed dramatically. The sad and shy little boy who came into my office just three months prior was now eager to share with me how he was doing and what was going on in his life. I asked Eric to tell me what things we had done that were the most helpful to him. He mentioned that he liked reading books, playing with the toys in my office, and drawing pictures. I asked him to draw one final picture that demonstrated his change; Eric drew a picture of his mother, himself, and his puppy playing outside.

In our last family session, Alice and Eric shared that they had visited the grave of their father/grandfather a few days before on his birthday. They shared that while they missed him every day, they liked to talk about how happy he would be with their progress. Each said that they talk about him frequently, and Eric often looked at his scrapbook and photo album. However, now there were new activities, new friends, and new interests in their lives. They both found enjoyment in the time they spent together and in independent activities. I encouraged them to continue what they had started.

After discussing how each could maintain their progress, we talked about our feelings about the termination. Alice stated that she was sad at losing the therapeutic relationship, but happy that she had "come so far." I told her how much I appre-

ciated her willingness to work toward her goals and her commitment to a maintenance plan. I told Eric that he would not be coming to see me anymore. His char-
acteristically six-year-old response was pleasing. He simply said "OK."

I then asked Alice to call me in three months to let me know how things were
going. She gladly agreed.

Evaluation of Practice

I evaluated the treatment process by monitoring goal achievement and asking Alice
regularly if therapy was helping, and if there were any new issues to address. For
Eric, the treatment process was revised from time to time, using drawings, reading,
play therapy, games, walks, and talking. My goal was to vary techniques and
match interventions with what seemed the most pressing issue each week. I evaluated treatment outcome by determining how satisfied Alice and Eric were with the
therapy process and by evaluating goal attainment. Termination occurred when all
were satisfied that they had achieved their goals. Follow-up occurred at three and six
months after termination. Alice called to tell me that things were continuing to go
smoothly.

Questions

**The author presented an interesting, successfully terminated case that involved
many issues commonly found in mental health practice. Taking a broad view of
this case, reevaluate the author's work and your participation through the
questions asked throughout the case.**

**1. Overall, what is your professional opinion of the work performed in this
case? As always, refer to the professional literature, practice evidence, your
experience, and the experience of student-colleagues when developing your
opinion.**

**2. Based on this review, what additional or alternative approaches could
have been used with this case? That is, if you were the practitioner, how would
you have approached this case? Please explain and justify your approach.**

**3. What did this case demonstrate that you could use in other practice set-
tings. List the most important things you learned and how you can use these in
your practice career.**

Bibliography

American Psychiatric Association (2000). *Diagnostic and statistical manual of mental disorders*
(4th ed., TR). Washington, DC: Author.

Beck, A. T., Ward, C., Mendelson, M., Mock, J., & Erbaugh, J. (1961). An inventory for measuring depression. *Archives of General Psychiatry, 4,* 561–571.

Carr, Alan. (2003). *What works with children and adolescents?* New York: Brunner Routledge.

Cooper, M. G., & Lesser, J. G. (2002). *Clinical social work practice.* Boston: Allyn and Bacon.

Cowger, C. D. (1994). Assessing client strengths: Clinical assessment for client empowerment. *Social Work, 39,* 3, 262–267.

Johnson, J. L. (2004). *Fundamentals of substance abuse practice.* Pacific Grove, CA: Brooks/Cole.

National Association of Social Workers (2000). *Code of Ethics of the National Association of Social Workers.* Washington, DC: Author.

Stern, M. B. (2002). *Child friendly therapy.* New York: W.W. Norton and Co.

Vernon, A. (2004). *Counseling children and adolescents.* Denver, CO: Love Publishing Co.

Dee

Sharyl St. John

Dee: I was here with my stepson, several years ago. He was having problems in school and was tested for ADHD. My doctor suggested I come today. I have been working with my doctor trying to regulate my hormones. (Dee begins to cry.) I cry all the time and it is not getting any better.

Social Worker: (using soft, concerned tones) You're crying a great deal of the time? Your doctor thought counseling might help?

Dee: Yes, we've tried increasing my antidepressants. Now my migraines are getting worse and I have no sex drive.

Social Worker: (concerned) So, on top of the depression, you are suffering with migraines and physical pain?

Dee: Yes, and I can't sleep at night. All I want to do is sleep during the day. I am yelling at everyone. Everyone seems to make me angry. (She wipes her eyes.) Just seeing Vern (client's stepson) or simply getting something to eat makes me want to scream.

Social Worker: Wow, you are having a great deal of emotion. It must be hard to manage your anger when you are so tired and having painful headaches.

This was the beginning of my therapeutic relationship with Dee. Some people believe that the most important part of the treatment process occurs in the beginning. That is, building an early alliance with clients is a critical part of successful treatment. According to O'Hanlon and Weiner-Davis (1989), successful treatment outcome occurs because of successful engagement during early treatment. Building a successful therapeutic relationship challenges practitioners to create an environment that wins clients' trust. Practitioners must learn to communicate competence, acceptance, and respect, along with interviewing skills such as probing, clarification, paraphrasing, reflection, active listening, reframing, and empathy, for this to occur.

> *Social Worker:*   (with empathy) How long have you been struggling with all of this?
>
> *Dee:*   It feels like forever, but I think I've been seeing my doctor for a year about the depression and headaches. He must hate seeing my name on his calendar. . . . I know I frustrate him. I just don't feel any better.
>
> *Social Worker:*   I know you must be suffering, don't worry about challenging your doctor. You are a strong, intelligent woman. I am sure he is concerned about failing you; it sounds like the two of you have a good professional relationship.

Dee's History

Identifying Information

When we met for the first time, Dee was a 37-year-old Caucasian female. She was barely five-foot tall and petite, with spiked, short platinum blonde hair. As she stated above, Dee's family physician referred her to me because her symptoms of depression were not responding to pharmaceutical treatment alone. She had been on 10 mg of a popular antidepressant, then 20 mg for six months. The mean dosage for this antidepressant is 20–40 mg. Her initial symptoms included weight gain, increased need for sleep, anger combined with radical mood swings, and prolonged bouts of crying. Just prior to our first meeting, her physician had switched Dee's medication and was examining her hormone levels to address menstruation irregularities. Despite these efforts, Dee reported minimal symptom relief. Her doctor requested a mental health diagnosis, mental health treatment if indicated, and a consultation from our agency psychiatrist regarding medication.

Presenting Problem

In addition to her ongoing problems with depression, Dee stated that her home environment was stressful, and that this stress impeded her recovery from depression. According to Dee, her main complaint at home pertained to her teenage son, Vern. She stated that her husband, Russ, had not disciplined Vern in years, leading to Vern becoming a belligerent and defiant teenager and a source of significant conflict in their marriage. Recently, school personnel suspended Vern for possession of marijuana. The school referred his case to the juvenile justice system. This was Vern's third suspension from school in six weeks. Dee feared that his continuing problems would eventually destroy her marriage. At the time of our meeting, Dee and Russ, along with two children—Vern, Dee's 16-year-old stepson, and Mark, Dee's 10-

year-old biological son from her second marriage—comprised her immediate family system.

Marital and Family History

Dee's marriage to Russ was her third. Her first marriage lasted less than one year due to her husband's recurrent substance abuse and domestic violence. She did not want to talk about this marriage much, given that it had ended twenty years earlier. However, she did offer some interesting information about that relationship. She married this man right after graduating high school. Dee said that they were too young to get married (Dee was 18 years old) because neither could handle the responsibility. She further reported that they spent most of their time in bars, drinking with friends. Many of these nights ended with arguments between them that sometimes turned violent. After one physical altercation and at the insistence of her family, Dee petitioned the courts for a restraining order against her spouse and filed for divorce. She did not know what had happened to her first husband after their marriage ended, since they had no further contact.

Dee began a relationship with her soon-to-be second husband soon after her divorce. Within three months, Dee moved in with him and became pregnant. Her second marriage lasted ten years, and they had three biological children. At the time of our meeting, her daughters were 21 and 17 years old, and her son Mark was 10 years old. Her second husband drank alcohol "a great deal," but their relationship never became violent. They had "other problems." She recalled that they often argued, something Dee believed happened because both had "type A personalities." She said that her second husband worked hard and played hard. He also had clear expectations how she should manage their home, how children should behave, and Dee's role as wife and mother. Dee eventually filed for divorce to gain her independence. She wanted to be alone in the world to discover "who she was."

Her pattern of moving rapidly from one relationship to the next continued after her second marriage. Dee met and married Russ six months after her second divorce, in an impromptu service in Las Vegas. When we first met, Dee and Russ had been married seven years. She said that her marriage to Russ had always been "good," except for their differences in parenting styles. Dee stated that she was "very strict" and had "high expectations" for her children. She went on to list her son Mark's academic achievements, his character strengths, and his goals for college. She stated that her oldest child was married with two children and her other daughter was a senior in high school. When she discussed Vern, she shared that he smoked cigarettes in his bedroom against house rules, was failing his classes, and had been repeatedly suspended from school for behavior problems. His last suspension was his first for using drugs. Dee stated that she had tried to discipline him, but Russ always overrode her punishment and let Vern "do as he pleased." Dee believed that she had no control over her situation and was angry that Vern's behaviors were destroying her marriage and family, and that she could not do anything about it.

Dee added that she was also satisfied with the school system. She believed that Vern "deserved every suspension he got" from the high school and the principal was "fair and firm." She only wished that the district provided in-house suspension because she did not believe that forcing Vern to stay home from school was "punishment." She was hoping that the juvenile justice system would punish Vern, but his case was still pending at the court.

Dee worked as a housekeeper at a local hospital. She stated that she "liked" her job, mainly because she did not have much contact with patients or staff. This allowed her to avoid the irritable "cliques" at the hospital. She added that she only socialized with one person at work. Dee also liked that her job gave her a daily break from the stress at home (mostly Vern) and served as a distraction from her depression. Since the family was financially well-off, Dee's income was hers to keep and use as she pleased. She liked having her own money to buy what she wanted without having to justify herself and her actions to her husband. Her future professional goals included completing a Certified Nurses Aid training program.

According to Dee, Russ owned and operated a successful carpet cleaning business that provided well for the family. They could afford whatever they wanted and needed. However, Dee stated that Russ often spent extravagantly, insisting on an expensive 5,000-square-foot home, providing each teenager with their own car, and buying an expensive cabin cruiser with a camper. They often "footed the bill" for travel with friends, which usually included expensive activities and costly parties. Dee stated that many of their current marital problems were partly because of Russ's extravagant spending and lifestyle.

Pertaining to social relationships, Dee did not have many friends, and this did not bother her. She sometimes socialized with one person from work. Russ and she occasionally played cards with another couple. When asked about her friendships, Dee stated that her friends did not appreciate her tendency to confront problems in a "tell-it-like-it-is" approach. Similar to her intimate relationships, she stated that her friends would rather ignore issues than deal with them directly.

Histories of Addiction: Dee's Families

In reviewing Dee's extended family, I discovered a long history of alcohol abuse. She knew little about her paternal grandfather, although she did recall her grandmother complaining because he would disappear for days on drinking binges. Dee stated that her father was a recovering alcoholic, with over 20 years of sobriety. Her father had stopped drinking without professional help. While she rarely saw her father drunk, she knew that he had a drinking problem. He was a difficult man to please and, according to Dee's recollection, alcohol made him easier to tolerate. However, she did recall hearing loud arguments between her parents, behind closed doors. She also recalled that her mother cried a lot when she was young.

While discussing her father, Dee became visibly angry and shared that he smoked heavily and was dying of emphysema. Since Dee worked in a hospital, she claimed to know how "awful" the dying process would be for her Dad, yet she stated that he would not listen to her and stop smoking. She said that her mother and sister never spoke about it because it might disrupt family harmony, so she felt alone in her mission to save her father from a long, painful death. Her efforts were not working, as her father continued to smoke and her mother and sister continued to ignore the issue.

Dee further shared that she often felt alienated from her family and frequently left family gatherings in fits of anger over differences of opinion. She was a person that "spoke her mind" while her family preferred to ignore family problems. As she matured, Dee's outspokenness challenged the long-standing, yet unspoken rule of "saving the family harmony" by challenging the behavior of family members. These disagreements often led to days or weeks of silence between family members. Finally, someone would call another, ending their arguments and beginning again the pattern of what Dee called an elaborate game of "pretend it never happened." Dee stated that the family had also played this "game" for years after her parents would loudly argue behind closed doors. That is, they acted as if nothing had happened and everything was fine, while everyone in the family "knew" about the arguments and father's drinking. Yet, nobody ever dared speak about these issues.

I wondered aloud whether this "game" occurred in her present marriage. Answering affirmatively, Dee stated that they also argued behind closed doors and "pretended" that it never happened. However, she stated that their pattern was different, because she confronted Russ about his unresponsiveness more readily than she did her family-of-origin. Moreover, Russ usually attributed his "lack of follow through" after an argument to his forgetfulness, instead of her father's usual, "I don't want to talk about it." To Dee, Russ—like her father—wanted to avoid disrupting family harmony, or more specifically the harmony between himself and Vern. Dee believed that Russ had a habit of "walking away from everything," especially his responsibilities toward Vern.

It appeared that Dee's family had a long history of chemical dependency and the resultant control issues, spanning at least three generations. Dee's presenting problems were characteristic of people that grew up in chemically dependent families. Dee's issues were a by-product of her family history and each member of her family struggled with the same issues. However, each demonstrated their problems differently through behaviors such as anger, control, rebellion, abuse of substances, as well as other self-defeating activities.

During our initial session, we also uncovered that Russ had chemical dependency in his background, again for at least three generations. His first wife (Vern's mother), died in an alcohol-related automobile accident when Vern was 2 years old, but Russ was not with her on the night of the accident. It also appeared that Russ might have a drinking problem of his own. Dee stated that Russ drank in the same way that he spent money, fast and hard. Yet, she qualified this statement by stating that she did not think he was alcoholic.

Dee also reported that both she and Russ had stopped drinking two years earlier. Concerning her own alcohol use, Dee stated that she never had experienced legal or professional problems, but she quit because she did not like how often or how much she was drinking or the "weekend hangovers." They decided to quit drinking following a series of serious marital disputes that turned violent. Dee recalled that Russ had thrown a telephone and a beer bottle at her on one occasion. During their last violent mishap, Russ had tried to choke her. She did not report this to local authorities. While Dee stated that she did not miss drinking, she did miss her friends from those years. Based on the description of her previous drinking pattern and her ability to stop drinking, I believed that Dee did not meet the criteria for alcohol dependence. On the other hand, Russ might be a different case. According to Dee, Russ continued to make occasional trips to see his old drinking friends and missed drinking with his friends. However, she stated that he "will not touch another drop," claiming that she would immediately leave if Russ ever drank again.

This presented the most significant ethical issue involved in this case. While I had concerns about Russ's drinking patterns, he was not my client. I believed that Russ at least should be part of Dee's treatment, but her Health Maintenance Organization (HMO) only approved her for individual therapy. Therefore, I could not treat them as a couple or family. My charge was to treat Dee individually, so I did not pursue this any further. Yet, as a professional practitioner, I knew she had relationship and family issues that would need addressing and that perhaps Russ needed individual help as well. This presented a significant dilemma throughout my relationship with Dee.

Questions

In the preceding paragraph, the author described her ethical dilemma about her inability to treat the couple, family, and/or Russ. In this age of managed care, where insurance companies and not on-site practitioners often make clinical decisions, this dilemma is common. As students preparing to practice at an advanced level, you will face this problem on a daily basis.

1. Research the current literature on managed care. When and for what reasons was managed care introduced into mental health practice?

2. How has managed care changed the way that practitioners must work with their clients? This can be stated in terms of treatment options, number of sessions or intensity of treatment, time management issues for practitioners, and/or the dilemma of having offsite decision makers making on-site clinical decisions, to name a few.

3. What is your opinion about how the author chose to rectify her managed care dilemma? When you find yourself in the same dilemma, what additional options would you consider beyond what the author stated?

Dee also believed that their excessive lifestyle had negatively affected Vern. Vern was 2 years old when his mother died, and was 16 when I met Dee. She believed that Russ tried to make-up for the loss of his mother by lavishing Vern with expensive toys. Over the years, Vern became used to receiving expensive toys and having fun weekends with intoxicated parental supervisors. This, she believed, created many of the problems Russ and she had over parenting styles in their marriage.

Dee's Symptoms and History of Depression

Near the end of our first session, Dee discussed her symptoms of depression. These included weight gain, bouts of anger, crying, and disrupted sleeping patterns. Dee's primary care physician had been treating her depression with medication. When asked about this, Dee stated that she liked her doctor and had been seeing him for years. However, in this instance, his treatment was not working and they both believed that she needed specialized attention. She also shared that her "depression" had been a problem for about one year. However, the stress added by Vern's behavior was making her depression "unmanageable." Besides the medication, Dee was trying to lose weight through a workout program at a local gym with an acquaintance from work. She hoped that counseling might help her learn to control her anger toward her stepson, improve her marriage, and relieve her depressive symptoms. She also hoped that changes in her medication would help with this process too.

Questions

Now that the author has presented Dee's history in significant detail, and before reading her clinical assessment and diagnoses below, perform the following exercises based on your education, experience, the professional literature, and best practice evidence. To increase the learning potential of this exercise, you may want to do this in a small group with other students.

1. Based on the information contained above, construct a three-generation genogram and eco-map that represents Dee's personal, familial, and environmental circumstances. What further information do you need to complete this exercise? What patterns do these two important graphical assessment tools demonstrate?

2. Write a comprehensive list of Dee's issues and strengths.

3. Write a two- to three-page narrative assessment that encompasses Dee's multi-systemic issues and strengths (review Chapter 1, if needed). This narrative should provide a comprehensive and multi-systemic explanation of her life as she prepares to undergo therapy with the author.

4. Try to identify the theoretical model or approach you use to guide your assessment. According to the literature, what other theoretical options are available, and how would these change the nature of your assessment?

5. Finish these exercises by developing multi-axial DSM-IV-TR diagnoses for Dee. Be sure to look for evidence of multiple diagnoses on Axis I. Provide

the list of client symptoms that you used to justify your diagnostic decisions. What, if any, information was missing that would make this an easier task?

Multi-Systemic Assessment and Initial Diagnosis

The DSM-IV-TR (2000) criteria for major depression require that five symptoms be "present during the same two-week period and representing a change from previous functioning" (pp. 161–162). During our first session, Dee reported the following symptoms:

1. Crying episodes
2. Decreased sexual interest
3. Increased anger and frustration
4. Atypical weight gain
5. Hypersomnia

Hence, her referring physician's diagnosis of major depressive disorder appeared accurate. I substantiated this diagnosis during our first interview. Furthermore, her doctor appeared to be addressing her medical needs through medication and health education. Her doctor also responded to concerns about her disrupted menstrual cycle by investigating hormone levels and fluctuations.

We identified Dee's family, marital, and social systems as the most pressing problems to consider in treatment. She identified problems with her stepson, her husband, and her extended family. She described the problems as her family's inability to face difficult issues and deal with them openly and justly. Her family-of-origin did not talk openly about her father's disease, or his certain death from smoking. Russ was unwilling to confront Vern about his behavioral problems or discipline him for his actions. These problems placed her at-risk for marital separation and divorce.

Dee identified her main personal strength as her ability to communicate. She believed that she was "emotionally strong," educated, and "straightforward" in all of her interpersonal exchanges. In contrast to her family, Dee stated that she "always" verbalized her feelings openly and supported her statements with facts that "proved she was right." During our sessions, she pointedly stated that she disliked Vern and provided examples of each disrespectful act he committed over the previous seven years. She listed each "positive" parenting choice she made and outlined Russ's failure to support her.

Dee limited her friendships to an acquaintance from work and one couple she and Russ played cards with occasionally. In her social relationships, her familial avoidance pattern discussed above repeated. Dee identified problems, expounded on the specifics, defined solutions, and became angry if people disagreed about her solution. It seemed that most people did not appreciate Dee's ability to be correct in most situations.

It appeared to me that Dee was unaware of the patterns and themes that coursed throughout her relationships. She also seemed unaware of the links between these patterns and her presenting problems. Dee stated that her main goal in treatment was to focus on Vern and his behavioral problems; she wanted to know how to get her husband to discipline the boy. If only he would do it the way she wanted, she was sure that her anger would subside and their marriage would improve. I believed it was not that simple.

Questions

Do you agree with the author's diagnosis of major depressive episode? Are there any additional factors that you would consider with Dee and her situation? For example, what role does the apparent history of alcohol dependence play in her life? What would be the best modalities (individual, group, family, etc.) for Dee's treatment? Defend your opinions and ideas from the professional literature, personal practice experience, and/or from information learned through discussion with student-colleagues.

Eco-Maps and Genograms

To help with my work, I constructed an eco-map to provide a pictorial perspective of the client's relationships with her husband, family, and other social support systems. Dee's eco-map highlighted key patterns and themes in her life. It also illustrated that Dee's depression fluctuated in relationship to the amount of personal power and control she believed that she possessed in any relationship. For example, when Dee was a consumer (doctor or fitness center), she experienced little conflict. She could easily define her role in these relationships and retain power as the "customer." In her work environment, Dee received financial rewards for providing a clearly defined service for the hospital. Moreover, she could avoid conflict because she did not have to interact with others in the hospital.

Her family and other social relationships were different. In her family-of-origin, Dee was frustrated. I assumed that her frustration was related to her felt need to be "close" to her family. This need often clashed with her desire to control their relationships and her inability to do so to the extent that she believed was necessary. Dee not only wanted to be in control, but she also wanted the people in her life to recognize her as being in control, that is, Dee wanted others to define and treat her as the one person with the appropriate wisdom and strength to solve everyone's problems. She craved respect; something she believed that she "never" earned in her youth. Her solution exacerbated her dilemma. When others ignored her opinion, she tried even harder to convince them that she was right, often leading to long periods of personal disconnection.

While Dee reported feeling close to her family, she also reported a history of conflict because family members did not share her ideas or goals. Dee stated that her main problem was Vern, primarily because she could not control his behavior.

Vern had become the major focus of Dee's stress. She reported feeling "trapped" by Vern. She could not remove herself from the relationship by "going home," as she could when her family-of-origin, friends, and coworkers bothered her. Moreover, Vern did not conform to her interpretation of what a teenager should embody. The more Vern caused trouble, the less Dee believed she had control over his behaviors. This realization exacerbated her stress levels, leading to more severe symptoms of depression. Her relationship with Russ complicated the pattern. Since he would not deal with Vern the way Dee wanted, she grew angry with him as well, causing her to question the appropriateness of her marriage. Hence, Dee became increasingly "dis-eased" in her family system and personal life. Medical issues, family issues, and relationship issues stressed her. She was having trouble accepting that she had minimal control over the people in her immediate environment and her depression caused her to be even less tolerant. She was trapped in a never-ending cycle that left her feeling depressed, frustrated, and angry.

Dee's genogram illustrated an additional feature in her life—substance abuse. Family practitioners often use genograms to detect recurrent patterns in a family system across generations. It diagrams the names, birth order, gender, and relationship patterns of family members and significant others across at least three generations of a family system. Alcohol dependence occurred in each generation and affected each family member in the system. Dee's paternal grandfather was a heavy drinker and her father was a recovering alcoholic. Dee had been married to three men with alcoholic tendencies and was a recovering substance abuser herself. Now, she had a stepson with substance abuse issues. Numerous studies suggest that alcoholics, and those raised in alcoholic homes, share certain characteristics (Twerski, 1997). It is unclear whether physiology, psychology, or social factors are responsible for these factors, but Twerski (1997) suggests that these factors include rationalization, manipulation, rigidity of thought, emotional hypersensitivity, increased sense of victimization, and anger. It appeared to me that Dee demonstrated many of these characteristics.

In the context of the family, Dee saw herself as "the voice of reason." That is, she knew her family's problems and believed that she knew the correct way to fix their problems, if Russ and Vern would only listen. I believed that this issue represented the different roles that Dee assumed as a child. In her family-of-origin, Dee had become the fixer, leader, and healer. Dee's family had a long history of chemical dependency and control issues. She grew up in an environment of parental control and denial. She countered this by marrying a man (her first husband) who offered no structure or pretense of protecting "harmony" in the relationship. Dee's second husband provided a path back to her family-of-origin. He was controlling like her father, and he used alcohol to soften his otherwise perfectionist personal style.

When she married Russ, Dee reassumed her role as "leader" and "fixer." For example, Dee believed she was correct in all situations. During a disagreement, she would provide supporting data for her opinions about how things should go, and then rationalize her decisions and manipulate those around her into agreement. With her father, Dee cited medical knowledge and personal experience as the reason for her continual insistence that he quit smoking. She similarly felt justified in pre-scribing how Russ should handle Vern. The stories about the successes of her bio-logical children validated, in Dee's mind, that she knew what she was talking about and Vern's problems "proved" that Russ did not.

Additionally, Dee could not see so-called gray areas. She believed that life was "either-or," or "black or white." Her father either stopped smoking or died. Russ either disciplined Vern her way or Vern would fail. She was right and others were wrong, misinformed, or simply lazy and uninterested. Her approach to relationships had caused her great misery, and I believed played a significant role in her present-ing problems.

Another tactic used by people from alcoholic family backgrounds, and one that had a significant affect on Dee's situation, was the defense tactic known as pro-jection. Twerski (1997) defines projection as the psychological process of blaming other people or circumstances for one's problems. Projection relieves people from having to take responsibility for themselves and their behaviors, as well as from having to make changes. Dee projected the source of her personal problems onto those closest to her, allowing her to remain unaccountable for her problems. She also believed that her problems would disappear if when others around her changed. For example, Dee believed that Russ was to blame for Vern's behavior because he refused to discipline him properly. She offered as "proof" the fact that Vern con-stantly violated the rules at school and at home. Therefore, Russ's inattention to Vern caused problems at home, and made her depressed and angry. Because of them, she had to attend therapy to change their behavior. She made it clear that her problems were their fault, and that they needed to change, not her.

Questions

The author assumes an approach based on the belief that chemical dependen-cy is a disease and that all family members suffer from this disease. Her posi-tion is that addiction is the overriding issue in people's lives, whether it is the addicted person or their family members. Hence, the author's narrative assess-ment, or her definition of Dee's problems, flows directly from this belief. Some have called this constellation of behaviors codependency (Johnson, 2004). Therefore,

1. **Explore the professional literature regarding addiction and its impact on family members as children and later in adulthood. From what literature or theoretical background is the author basing her beliefs and practices with Dee? Based on your reading of the literature, what is your professional position on these theories as the basis for mental health treatment?**

2. **The author appears to believe that Dee's need to control relationships is central to her problems. First, what is your position on this issue? Use the pro-fessional literature or other practice evidence to justify your position. Second, are there other ways to define Dee's problems and personal style that provides**

alternative definitions of her presentation? If so, how would the alternative definitions affect treatment delivery?

3. Now that you have written a narrative assessment and have read the author's narrative assessment, it is time for you to plan treatment. Given what you know about depression, develop a treatment plan for Dee based on the theoretical approach that you prefer when working with depressed individuals and/or families. Please give a written and detailed rationale for your decision making regarding this case.

Treatment Planning

To develop a treatment plan, I asked Dee a series of questions about her life in hopes of formulating ideas about her treatment needs. While this process began as my effort to plan treatment, over time I needed to make treatment planning a collaborative effort with Dee. To be successful, treatment planning must be a joint effort between client and practitioner. I typically introduce treatment planning to clients as a "roadmap" designed to guide treatment and help keep client and practitioner on course toward goal achievement. This is how Dee and I discussed this issue.

Dee's focus at the beginning of therapy was to force Russ into disciplining Vern the way she thought parents should discipline wayward adolescents. If she could achieve that goal, Dee believed that her personal symptoms would disappear. Therefore, our first treatment goal was to "reduce Dee's anger and rage." As a practitioner, I looked for information during the assessment demonstrating any behavior pattern that might aggravate or initiate Dee's presenting symptoms of depression. That is, I searched for underlying dynamics that helped create the context where her symptoms would surface.

Questions

The author refers to a psychodynamic approach. These theories focus on the internal workings and makeup of clients in assessing problems and planning change. The popularity of these approaches has waxed and waned over the years. However, despite the current popularity of different approaches (i.e., solution-focused, systems interventions, etc.) psychodynamic theory continues to inform practitioners.

1. Using the professional literature and information from other courses, define and discuss the basis of psychodynamic therapies, and contrast it with other theories outside the psychodynamic theoretical "family."

2. What other approaches do you believe may be appropriate for working with a client with Dee's presentation and life history?

As stated earlier, Dee had a long history with personal and familial alcohol use and she demonstrated many of the characteristic personality traits often accompanying people from chemically dependent families, including anger, rigid thinking, manipulation, rationalization, and projection. As illustrated by her genogram and eco-map, these traits manifested in her immediate family and other intimate relationship systems across her life span. Based on the theoretical approach mentioned above, I assumed that these traits created personal conflict and helped maintain Dee's symptoms. I also assumed that these traits contributed to her problems in the past and would continue to be problematic if they went unidentified. Therefore, our second treatment goal was to increase Dee's awareness of the underlying issues that helped create family and relationship problems past and present.

Questions

Now that you have read the author's assessment and treatment plan, as well as having developed your own assessment and treatment plan,

1. How does your assessment and treatment plan compare to the author's? Locate and explore areas of similarity and difference between them.

2. Discuss the differences and provide a rationale from the professional literature, practice evidence in the field, your experience in similar client situations, and/or from discussion with student-peers in the classroom.

3. Based on your conclusions from 1 and 2 above, if you were Dee's therapist, what course of action would you use going forward? Defend your decisions.

Dee's Treatment

In the early 1980s, psychotherapy began shifting away from psychodynamic theories. Clinicians such as William O'Hanlon and Michele Weiner-Davis (1989), along with Saleebey (2002) and others promoted an emphasis on client strengths and change rather than pathology and deficits. These authors believed that these shifts in emphasis could negate the need for long-term therapy and provide better clinical outcomes for clients. Health Maintenance Organizations (HMOs) jumped on the bandwagon and, in an effort to reduce costs, in the mid to late 1980s began limiting outpatient therapy to six to eight sessions. This shift marked the end of prolonged outpatient therapy, unless clients paid for services privately. The "new" approaches were solution-focused and strengths-based, instead of long-term, insight-oriented psychodynamic approaches. Proponents of solution-focused approaches emphasized the need for change to ease or solve client problems, regardless of whether clients gained insight into, or understood the origins of their problems. The treatment plan we developed for Dee coordinated well with solution-based and psycho-dynamic approaches. Dee's perspective of her problems and her reactions to them would need to change in order to reduce her symptoms of depression. However, she would also have to change what she did, looking for new ways to behave that "worked" better for her in daily life.

Employing empathy, active listening, and reframing, I asked Dee about her various efforts "to help Russ parent Vern." As she described her lengthy and tiresome attempts to help him, I tried to establish rapport by demonstrating that I understood her feelings and frustrations. That is, at this stage of our relationship, I did not confront or challenge her attitudes, feelings, or behaviors. My task was to understand them to the best of my ability.

Dee tried being the disciplinarian; she offered suggestions to Russ about what he should do when Vern broke the rules, and helped enforce whatever consequences Russ imposed on Vern. Moreover, Dee yelled at Russ and Vern, withdrew her attention from them, and even threatened to divorce Russ if "things didn't change." She also tried to get Russ to participate in family counseling. Nothing seemed to motivate Russ into action.

She stopped cooking for Vern and refused to do his laundry, hoping he would "get the message" of her disapproval of his actions in the home. Evidently, Dee worked hard to correct Vern's misbehaviors by badgering Russ to take parental action. She would extend the same intensity toward extended family, friends, and coworkers when they behaved inappropriately. As stated earlier, Dee cited several attempts to get her father to stop smoking, to no avail.

Dee also had "major" problems with how Russ handled their income taxes. His handling of the finances, especially the income taxes, had been a source of continual confrontation in their marriage. Dee would argue with him over his willingness to allow unpaid business taxes to "pile up" year after year. She even scheduled appointments with professional income tax preparers, and finally, when that did not work, refused to participate in the financial management of Russ's business.

I aligned with Dee on her arduous task of holding her loved ones' to high moral standards and out of harm's way. I affirmed her strength and fortitude as demonstrated by her attempts to solve her family's problems. My goal was to focus early treatment sessions on Dee's behaviors, her approach to problem solving, and her strengths. This strategy laid the groundwork for the next phase of treatment. It was time to discuss which of her helping attempts had worked, what solution-focused practitioners call identifying exceptions to the problem (Peller & Walter, 1992).

O'Hanlon and Weiner-Davis (1989) state that "the exception question directs the client to search in the present and the past rather than the future for solutions by focusing on those times when clients do not or have not had their problems even though they expected they would" (p. 24). This query allows practitioners to support their clients in their search for solutions that have already worked. That is, this exercise helps clients tap their inherent strengths and resources that they may not consciously recognize they possess.

Social Worker: You have tried to help, you have tried to punish, you have offered to participate in counseling, and you have tried to ignore the problems. Dee, you have worked so hard. Has anything helped?

Dee: Boy, you would think so, but it hasn't.

Social Worker: With Russ and the taxes, you tried to help. It sounds like you tried to get professional help and finally just gave up.

Dee: Yes, it was useless.

Social Worker: How does it feel now, now that you no longer get involved in the taxes?

Dee: I am less stressed. I may have moments of anger, but then I talk to myself and walk away. At least we are not fighting about it any more.

Social Worker: So you tried to change the situation in every possible way, and then decided that the only approach was to let it go, let Russ do it his way. What I also hear is that you can talk to yourself, remind yourself, to walk away from the situation and that this helps you calm down.

Dee: Yes.

This is called presupposition questioning. O'Hanlon and Weiner-Davis (1989) believe that presupposition questioning functions as an information-gathering tool and "intervention" (p. 79). Its intent is to influence the client's perceptions in the direction of solutions, instead of problems. I wanted to intervene by shifting Dee away from discussing her problems to a focus on change. This line of questioning also emphasizes the "self-enhancing and strength-promoting" qualities in a client's personal repertoire (O'Hanlon & Weiner-Davis, 1989, p. 80).

Dee could not identify a workable solution to Russ's income tax problem. However, she did realize that "staying out" of his tax situation reduced her stress. Prior to this, Dee stated that she was in continual fear of an IRS audit and was constantly frustrated with him. This had gone on for over two years. She believed that he chose to remain in denial about the seriousness of unpaid back taxes. In her typical pattern, she listed the facts of the situation and tax laws, threatened him, problem-solved, and when that did not work, stopped trying to help. The last option, as it turned out, was the solution that had given her the most relief. While Russ did not change, she found that her anger and stress diminished.

Social Worker: With Russ, you tried to solve the problem, but he just wasn't willing to make any changes in his approach to filing taxes. So, you stopped trying to change him and your stress and anger reduced. Do you think it might help if you stopped getting involved in Vern's problems and left them up to Russ to resolve?

Dee: I might feel better, but then I will eventually have to pick up the pieces of the mess they create, like with the law.

Social Worker: What do you imagine would happen if you did not get involved in Vern's discipline?

Dee: He'll continue to screw up. He'll get kicked out of school and I'll have to have him around the house all day.

Social Worker: How is that any different than what is happening now?

Dee: (laughing) I guess it isn't. But what if he doesn't graduate or ends up arrested?

Social Worker: Can you assure that he will go to school, get adequate grades, and graduate. Can you watch over him all the time to guarantee that he will not get in trouble and get arrested.

Dee: No.

Social Worker: If he fails to finish school or ends up in jail, who's fault is it?

Dee: His.

Social Worker: Who will pay the consequences for these behaviors?

Dee: Well it could be me. I might have to pay the legal fees or I could get stuck having him live with me longer because he doesn't graduate.

Social Worker: That is one choice you have. But, you could also choose to have him pay his own legal fees, or even spend some time in detention. He would have to pay his own consequences.

Dee: (laughing) At eighteen I could tell him to move out?

Social Worker: Yes, that is a choice you have.

Dee: I could just let them do what they want to do and not get involved. If he gets into trouble, Russ can figure it out. (pauses) I like that.

Dr. William Glasser is a strong proponent of Choice Therapy and Reality Therapy (What Is Reality Therapy? 2003). The three major components of this model are, practitioners must create a trusting environment for their client, examine client needs, and create a plan to satisfy those needs that clients choose to enact. By this time, Dee and I had established a strong therapeutic alliance. She had identified her goal and seemed prepared to work toward achieving it. In the dialogue described above, Dee could identify possible solutions to her problem; one that she could facilitate. Choice Therapy contends that people can only control their own behavior, not the behavior of others. Dee's original hope was to change Russ and Vern. However, during therapy Dee learned that she could meet her own needs (symptom relief) by changing only her own behavior in relation to Russ and Vern. When she accomplished that, she experienced fewer symptoms of depression, anger, and rage. That is, her depressive symptoms abated.

In our next session, we continued focusing on exceptions. Dee had separated herself from the business finances and refused to discuss it with him. The business taxes were now Russ's "business," not Dee's. She refused to participate in any conversation about the taxes, even when he brought it up. Interestingly, Dee had simultaneously removed herself from other stressful situations as well. She recalled a time when a coworker and herself had set up an exercise date at a local club. Her coworker failed to attend on two occasions, and this angered Dee immensely. She attempted to discuss this with her friend, to no avail. Then, Dee decided to attend the exercise class alone, and if her friend attended, fine. If not, at least Dee got to exercise.

I explored with Dee how she decided on this course of action. This line of questioning tried to identify Dee's underlying, internal messages. After some thought, Dee figured that she benefited from exercise and was unwilling to forfeit her health or well-being because her friend did not show up for class. We compared her reaction in that instance and her reaction to Russ's tax issues to how she handled Russ's parenting and Vern's behavior. After some conversation, Dee concluded that perhaps she should take the same approach toward Russ's parenting. Further, she concluded that there were times when she could not change other people.

When she was able to internalize her limitations in affecting change in other people, Dee found alternative ways to get her needs met, that did not include changing others to reach her goal. Her solution came from within, based on her own actions in similar situations in the past. Dee was not aware that she could try alternative solutions in her immediate family and get positive results. Together, Dee and I summarized this process in the following manner:

1. Dee identified a problem and became frustrated.
2. She asked for the situation to change by offering a solution. She became angry when others did not follow her advice.
3. Dee continued offering advice several times. Each time her advice was not followed, she became more frustrated and angry.
4. Dee figured out how to remove herself from the problem situation.
5. Dee's frustration and anger subsided.

At the beginning of our next session, Dee reported significant relief along with a sense of increasing hope because of the newfound solutions to her problems with others. On a scale of one to ten, with ten representing the most productive and one the least productive, Dee stated that her new solutions were a "nine." The use of self-reporting scales helps practitioners evaluate treatment progress and allows clients the opportunity to focus on their growth (O'Hanlon & Weiner-Davis, 1989). Scaling allows clients to "measure" their subjective feelings. At an individual level, it appeared that the process of change had begun.

Family Systems-Level Change

Now that Dee was making individual progress, I thought it appropriate to examine Dee's family system in an effort to identify information about her relationships in the past and how these patterns were reenacted in her present family. Dee learned that she did reenact many of the same behavioral patterns learned during her child-hood. She also figured that regardless of the problem, Dee had the "power" to exer-cise her right to step away from the situation and reduce her frustration level.

As treatment progressed, Dee began removing herself from the "problems" with Vern. In the two weeks between sessions, Dee identified several situations where she chose to ignore "Vern's problems." School personnel suspended Vern again for swearing at a teacher. The school telephoned her to pick Vern up at school. She called Russ at work and had him pick Vern up from the principal's office. Russ became "very unhappy" with this request. In fact, he "hung up" on her. However, Russ did pick Vern up from school.

According to systems theory, Dee and Russ's exchanges were important. Systems theory emphasizes, among other things, relationships and communication patterns. Practitioners help members to interact differently to treat problems indi-rectly. When members interact differently, the system must change as a result. This was happening in Dee's family. In her effort to reduce her frustration, Dee changed the way she interacted with Russ and Vern, creating an overall change in her fami-ly system. Instead of continuing to manage all the problems with Vern, she passed them off to Russ. For example,

> *Social Worker:*   Why do you think Russ hung up on you?
>
> *Dee:*   Because he was angry.
>
> *Social Worker:*   Why would he be angry with you? It was Vern who did something wrong.
>
> *Dee:*   Yes, but I have always taken care of it. I'm the one who has to be inter-rupted; I'm the one who has to drop everything and go pick him up. I have to call the courts to find out what to do with his drug charge. I have to pick him up from detentions.
>
> *Social Worker:*   So things have changed?
>
> *Dee:*   (adamantly) Oh, yea!

Dee's changes were disrupting the family's homeostasis, or status quo. She changed how she approached problems and left Russ and Vern to figure things out. By hanging up the phone, Russ attempted to reinstate the status quo, hoping Dee would react by stepping in to address the problems with Vern at school. However, Dee established new family rules and boundaries. She changed the interactional rules from Dee becoming angry, but handling the problems anyhow, to Dee leaving the problems for Russ to handle. She learned that she could not say "no" and still take care of the problem. This let Russ "off the hook," and increased the intensity of her symptoms.

Establishing new boundaries can be difficult for families, especially when the new boundaries represent a change from normal family functioning. Dee's family-of-origin organized around meeting her father's needs, first and always. Growing up, she learned to conform to his requests and expectations, as did the other women in the household. As an adult, Dee tested these unspoken rules, to no avail. When her father failed to heed her advice, Dee reverted to silence and denied her feelings. This led her into depression. As a result, Dee experienced several years of unspoken anger and resentment. She reenacted this learned role in her relationship with Russ. Dee similarly conceded to Russ's needs. The only difference between her marriage and family-of-origin was that Dee vocalized her anger and often raged at Russ and Vern, instead of remaining quiet. Hence, she lived with years of stockpiled anger and resentment, first from her family-of-origin, compounded by her marriage. In the exchange with Russ discussed above, Dee refused to sacrifice her day in order to take care of Vern or Russ. This made Russ angry.

Social Worker: Are you and Russ OK now?

Dee: Yes, he got over it. He came home, threw his keys down, and told me he didn't have time to pick Vern up from school during the day. It was funny because I told him to tell Vern that. He didn't like that either and stomped around the house for a while, but he got over it, and I stayed relaxed. I didn't even say anything to Vern. I figured it is not my problem.

Social Worker: So would you say you've found a way to reduce your anger?

Dee: Oh, yes.

In the following weeks, Dee continued practicing her new behaviors. She stopped trying to get Vern and Mark, her youngest son, to clean their room. She simply established a rule that the boys could not have food or drinks in their rooms. Instead of constantly arguing with them over their mess, Dee simply kept their bedroom doors closed so she did not have to see the mess. Laughing, she also established a new laundry policy. The boys had to deliver their laundry to her on laundry day. If they did not deliver, their laundry went undone. Mark began cleaning his room and bringing his laundry to the basement. Vern did not comply. According to Dee, Vern was now waiting for his clothes, washing them himself, or wearing dirty clothes to school.

Social Worker: So what would you say the consequence is for not cleaning their room?

Dee: They don't pick up their clothes, they don't get them washed.

Social Worker: And who suffers?

Dee: They do; the last thing these boys want is to have to do their own wash. Vern is so lazy, I don't think he even knows how to run the machine and he is almost an adult. Can you believe that?

Social Worker: Sometimes people change, or learn more, if they have to actually live the consequences.

Dee: Yes, I think Mark is learning the value of picking up his room. He sees that a clean room also means having clean clothes. But he doesn't like not being able to take food to his room. And Vern hasn't been suspended since the last time we met. I don't know if it was because of Russ getting involved, and I don't really care, as long as he leaves me alone.

Questions

The author discussed her therapy with Dee in the context of family systems theory. This theory suggests that changes in any part of a system forces change in others. That is, if one person changes, others must adjust to account for these changes. This process can cause severe disruption in families, including members becoming symptomatic that were not previously. This appears to be the case with Dee's family system. The family therapy literature often is the best place to find information about the application of systems theory in practice.

1. Review the professional literature about systems theory and its application with clients. Describe the major tenets of this approach, as it pertains specifically to its efficacy in therapy. What must practitioners know or be aware of while implementing change at the systemic level? According to the theory, is it possible to implement change that does not affect the larger system? Defend your answers using information from the practice literature.

2. Based on what you know at this moment about Dee's case, what steps would you take to account for the apparent changes that Russ is experiencing as Dee changes in relation to him? Defend your decisions with information from the literature, personal experience, and/or discussion with colleagues in class.

Mobilizing Additional Resources in Treatment

Her primary care physician initially referred Dee for therapy. During the initial assessment, Dee stated that she had a good relationship with her doctor and wanted him to continue treating her depression. Therefore, it was important that I maintain a direct line of communication with him during treatment. I sent her doctor a letter after our first session confirming that Dee had kept her appointment and that we were developing a treatment plan that included continuation of care with him, a psychiatric consultation, and individual therapy. The letter also confirmed the DSM-IV diagnosis of major depression.

However, our psychiatrist changed Dee's diagnosis. The consulting psychiatrist discovered that Dee actually had Bipolar Affective Disorder, Type II. The mental health exam revealed periods of highs and lows dating back to Dee's teen years. Years of alcohol abuse had muted her mood fluctuations. Only recently had Dee experienced racing thoughts and the "type A personality traits" common with this diagnosis.

While minimally altering the mental health treatment plan, the change of diagnosis drastically altered her pharmaceutical treatment. In clients with Bipolar Disorder, Type II, using antidepressants alone can incite episodes of mania. The most common treatment for bipolar disorder is anti-mania drugs. Researchers are also testing these drugs to treat aggression and rage. Therefore, the consulting psychiatrist began Dee on a trial of a common anti-mania drug at 25 mg. He added this drug to her current antidepressant medication to stabilize Dee's moods and help her lose weight. The antidepressant Dee used also caused sexual side effects, so the psychiatrist added another drug at a low dose to reverse this disturbing side effect.

Social workers play an important role in the diagnostic and treatment process, since many psychological symptoms treated in mental health clinics also have biological roots (Ginsberg, Nackerud, & Larrison, 2004). Dee's psychological concerns were part of a medical condition that required pharmaceutical treatment. With medication, her moods stabilized. My work with Dee helped her deal with the affects of her illness on her life and relationships.

I also referred Dee to a local Al-Anon group to learn more about the effects of alcoholism in the family system. Al-Anon is a support group adapted from Alcoholics Anonymous and is based on the twelve steps. Its purpose is to help families and friends of alcoholics recover from the affects of living with an alcoholic relative, partner, or friend. The affects may include low self-esteem, avoidance of feeling, overdeveloped sense of responsibility, compulsive personality traits, perpetual victim stance, or codependency (Johnson, 2004). Dee's overdeveloped sense of responsibility for the people in her family repeated over the course of treatment. Her most prominent emotion was anger, which hindered the development of interpersonal relationships.

One key concept of Al-Anon is detachment, or learning that one cannot control others. Fortunately, detachment was consistent with our work in therapy. Her friends and colleagues in Al-Anon supported any changes Dee began making in therapy. Over time, Dee began to master the skill of detaching from Russ or Vern. She learned to identify her needs and find solutions that did not require behavior changes in other members of the family. The support of a local group helped her maintain this new behavior, provide additional skills, and offer her a social support network.

Termination

Therapists who seek a "total cure" are in jeopardy of keeping their clients in treatment forever. I did not want to keep Dee as a client any longer than she minimally needed. The goal of therapy is to foster autonomy in life, not dependence on therapy. The managed care system reinforces this goal. In Dee's case, her HMO originally authorized eight individual therapy sessions. We used six. At the end of treatment, Dee had achieved the following:

1. She had gained a psychiatrist in her medical support system and an accurate diagnosis. The medication had greatly reduced symptoms of her mood disorder.
2. She had established a connection with a support group and increased the amount of time she spent on her own personal care, including physical exercise, a weight-loss program, and Al-Anon meetings.
3. She had learned how she dealt with problems in the past and identified new methods that worked in her current life.
4. She identified that she always sacrificed her needs to please others leading to unresolved anger and stress.
5. She achieved her goal of reducing her anger, frustration, and symptoms of depression.
6. She reported sleeping well after a medication change. She also reported that her moods had stabilized.
7. She began keeping a journal to track her moods. She identified her symptoms, rated each symptom on a scale of one to ten, and took steps to resolve her symptoms.
8. She began treatment near an eight on her self-report scale, where one indicated no symptoms and ten maximum symptoms. At the termination, Dee rated her symptoms a four or five.

At this stage, we decided to terminate this phase of therapy. Dee confirmed that she would call for support if any of her problems rose above an eight on her scale, or if the problems in her family intensified.

Questions

1. Take a moment to review Dee's progress in treatment. Based on the author's description, the professional literature, and the latest practice evidence, what occurred to account for her progress?

2. What was the theoretical approach or combination of approaches that appeared to work best for Dee?

3. Based on the work you have done earlier, what additional intervention(s) would you recommend? Use the literature and latest evidence to justify your recommendations.

Subsequent Treatment

I like to think of therapy as a road trip. People set out with a goal and create a map or plan to reach their destination. Along the way, they often encounter yields, cautions, and stops. Sometimes, they must turn around or stop to rest. In Dee's case, she hit an obstruction in the road. The obstruction was Russ.

As Dee continued to detach from Russ's behaviors, he became increasingly anxious and angry. He attempted to sabotage her Al-Anon meetings by denouncing the organization and belittling Dee for needing "support." He scheduled conflicting appointments to disrupt her meeting attendance, and tried to use anger to punish Dee. However, when he returned to drinking, Dee decided to return to therapy for support and assistance. The following exchange occurred in our first session together:

Dee: He told me he was getting something to eat with the people from work. I knew he was stressed out, he'd been short with all of us at home. He was working late a great deal. I thought the night with the guys would be good for him. I never expected he'd drink. I can't believe it. I told him I would leave him if he ever drank again (crying). I have to leave him, but I don't know how.

Social Worker: Oh, Dee (genuinely), how disappointing. I am so sorry.

Dee: I can't believe he did it. He would rather drink than be married. He knows I'll leave and he doesn't care. The marriage is over.

Social Worker: Did he say the marriage was over?

Dee: No, but I told him I would leave if he ever drank again. I don't know what I'll do. I'll have to find a second job, I'll lose the house (sobbing). I might even have to pay for half of the back taxes. I'll be bankrupt.

Social Worker: Dee, (softly) he relapsed, it was a relapse (gently touching her hand). You don't have to end the marriage because he relapsed. You don't have to do anything. You have many choices. What did your group say about this?

Dee: I haven't been in two weeks, I didn't call them (continuing to cry).

Social Worker: Dee, you need to use your call list. You need your group. They don't care if you've missed two weeks; they have been where you are today. They know about busy schedules, they know about relapse. You need to call the first person on the list, and if that person isn't available, then you call the next one and you continue to make phone calls until you reach someone.

Dee: (continuing to cry) How am I going to tell Mark? He thinks of Russ as a Dad, how could I do this to him again.

Social Worker: You aren't doing anything to Mark. Dee, you don't have to do anything right now with the marriage. Even if you decide to leave Russ, you didn't do it to Mark, Russ did.

There is always risk when one member of a family system changes without helping other members to change simultaneously. This risks upsetting family functioning to the point where one member might escalate his or her behavior in reaction to the unwanted or unplanned changes. The goal is to return the family to its old way of functioning, by creating a crisis that must be solved.

As Dee became healthier and "detached" from the problems between Russ and Vern, Russ became responsible for the problem. As the responsibilities shifted, Russ grew increasingly anxious. Obviously, when Russ quit drinking, he did not replace drinking with healthier coping skills. Dee accurately detailed each attempt he made to bring her back into the old relationship pattern. However, she did not detour from her plan. Consequently, Russ began coping by drinking.

Dee's HMO authorized four additional sessions for therapy. We used these sessions to educate and offer Dee insight. We used one session to illustrate how her family functioned as a system, with a predictable pattern. It illuminated how Dee's changes in behavior affected the entire family. We also revisited the concept of detachment. This time we emphasized detaching from Russ's drinking. Dee did not cause him to drink, nor could she control his drinking or cure his dependence. Finally, Dee was encouraged to continue utilizing the support of Al-Anon. The group represented an opportunity to widen her social circle with healthy adults and provide education and support in her current situation.

Russ's alcoholism quickly escalated. However, Dee's insurance did not have an ongoing "preventive care" benefit. The HMO explained that Dee's coverage was for crisis management, not ongoing illness. They reviewed with me that Dee reported her original symptoms resolved; she was no longer incurring sleep problems, crying, overeating, or having episodes of rage. She reported to the provider that her psychiatric care and medication were satisfactory. She reported using exercise and diet to return to her baseline weight and was involved in a support group. The provider concluded that her crisis was resolved. They decided that further treatment was "preventive" or "ongoing," neither of which her insurance covered. Thus, the HMO declared that any discomfort Dee reported was due to her continuing to live with an active alcoholic. Therefore, she could not remain in therapy.

This unfortunate turn of events demonstrates the need to begin the termination process during the first session. Insurance providers dictate the course of treatment for both mental and physical health care. By discussing this issue in the first session, we prepared Dee for the end of therapy. I offered a sliding scale fee based on her income, so she could continue on an "as-needed" basis.

In the End

Dee developed increased personal strength. She left with a list of self-help books to read and review. Most importantly, Dee increased her social support system. She managed her crisis without additional medication, in six sessions. We spaced these sessions every three to four weeks. At the conclusion of treatment, Dee's husband was in an intensive outpatient treatment program for his drinking that included family therapy. My time with Dee was complete.

Questions

The author presented an interesting case that involved many issues commonly found in mental health practice. Taking a broad view of this case, reevaluate the author's work and your participation through the questions asked throughout the case.

1. Overall, what is your professional opinion of the work performed in this case? As always, refer to the professional literature, practice evidence, your experience, and the experience of student-colleagues when developing your opinion.

2. Based on this review, what else could practitioners have done in this case? If you were the practitioner, how would you have approached this case? Please explain and justify your approach.

3. What could the author have done to deal more specifically with the changes in Russ? Given that Russ was technically not the author's client, should she have done anything at all?

4. What did this case demonstrate that you could use in other practice settings. List the most important things you learned and how you can use them in your practice career.

Bibliography

American Psychiatric Association (2000). *Diagnostic and statistical manual of mental disorders* (4th ed., TR). Washington, DC: Author.

Ginsberg, L., Nackerud, L., & Larrison, C. R. (2004). *Human biology for social workers: Development, genetics, and health.* Boston: Allyn and Bacon.

Johnson, J. L. (2004). *Fundamentals of substance abuse practice.* Pacific Grove, CA: Brooks/Cole.

O'Hanlon, W., & Weiner-Davis, M. (1989). *In search of solutions.* New York: W.W. Norton.

Peller, J., & Walter, J. (1992). *Becoming solution-focused in brief therapy.* New York: Brunner/Mazel.

Saleebey, D. (2002). *The strengths perspective in social work practice* (3rd ed.). Boston: Allyn and Bacon.

Twerski, A. (1997). *Addictive thinking.* Center City, MN: Hazelden.

What Is Reality Therapy? (2003). [online]. Available: http://indigo.ie/-irti/whatis.htm.

Dan and Ellen

Rosalyn D. Baker

This case involved a young, newly married couple struggling with marital discord revolving around the birth of their first child. They entered therapy wanting help with communication and division of labor in their home. What began as a relatively simple case of marital therapy evolved into a difficult, long-term, multifaceted treatment involving multiple mental health diagnoses, short-term spousal abuse, and individual and marital therapy covering nearly four years of on and off again therapy. This case demonstrates the power and impact of depression and other disorders on people's lives, and the various social work roles and responsibilities when treating clients with mental disorders.

Presenting Problems

Dan (age 31) and his wife, Ellen (age 30), appeared in my office for their first session of marital counseling. Ellen's best friend, Kim, a former client, referred them for therapy. Because of the supportive referral, Ellen and Dan arrived in my office hopeful for a positive outcome to their marital problems.

As our first session began, I believed that I could engage this couple in therapy. Dan and Ellen seemed hopeful, too. The combination of word-of-mouth referral and client hopefulness created an environment for successful client engagement. Ellen appeared to be the driving force behind therapy, but Dan also appeared willing to cooperate. However, I doubted that he would have initiated counseling on his own. He seemed shy and withdrawn, while attempting to put on a brave and confident face. My goal during the initial session was to build rapport, collect personal history, and conduct an assessment.

Dan presented himself as a happily married man, frustrated by his wife's continuous nagging about his lack of responsibility with household chores. He said that he was on a winning softball team that, along with his work, took up a lot of his time and energy. His wife's nagging frustrated him because it depleted his energy and caused resentment. Ellen said that Dan occasionally flew into a rage and stomped off to withdraw and sulk for hours at a time.

Dan was an introverted, quiet, handsome, Caucasian male. He was a large man who resembled a "teddy bear." He dressed casually and clean. I noticed that Dan entered my office hesitantly, yet greeted me politely with a firm handshake. His presentation contradicted his hesitant and reserved body language. I wondered if he was trying to cover anxious or resistant feelings. Perhaps, he was simply shy or unsure about what happens in therapy.

Ellen was an attractive, petite blonde woman with an assertive, outspoken demeanor. She was obviously the spokesperson in their marriage since she often spoke for both her and Dan. She was forthright about the reason they needed help. Since their baby was born three months earlier, their arguments had "gotten nastier." The new baby was wonderful, but Dan was not very helpful. Ellen tried various tactics to involve him as a parent, to no avail. This frustrated Ellen, "causing" her to become angry with Dan and the couple to argue most days. Ellen revealed that her "approach" usually included loud yelling and scolding.

Dan said that he did not have the energy to satisfy Ellen's demands. What Ellen defined as "requests" for help, Dan interpreted as "demands" on his time, leading to his resentment toward her and, sometimes, the new baby. His usual response to her demands was to "shut down" and refuse to talk. Dan's withdrawal during arguments frustrated Ellen, who often followed him around the house yelling, while Dan simply refused to participate. The more she followed and yelled, the more Dan withdrew.

Prior to the birth of their child, Ellen worked full-time as a designer. When the baby was born, she changed to part-time when she realized that Dan could not handle caring for their baby. Dan worked long hours in the computer industry. Before their child came, he seemed more involved with Ellen. However, since the birth, he had withdrawn, leaving parenting and housework entirely to Ellen. Their battles over division of labor and parenting caused significant relationship stress, and brought them to therapy.

As they spoke, I wondered if my own strong, independent personality reminded Dan of Ellen. Since I needed to engage both in therapy, I hoped that my approach would not cause problems for Dan. I needed to monitor how Dan responded to me in session, and not join too closely with Ellen. I did not want Dan to feel as if we "ganged up" on him. If he perceived me as a demanding woman, he might withdraw from me the way he did Ellen, and leave therapy. I quickly considered whether a male therapist might be better suited for Dan. However, I decided to wait because our relationship seemed off to a good start. I would monitor the situation as our relationship progressed, and temper my style in an effort to avoid giving Dan the impression that Ellen and I were on the same side. Besides, Dan was not the only person in this marriage with problems. Both partners contributed to their present impasse.

As usual, during intake sessions, I performed a risk assessment. Since I was beginning to believe that Dan and/or Ellen might have depression, a risk assessment was mandatory. Depression is a painful and confusing experience that can lead to feelings of hopelessness and helplessness, causing an otherwise healthy person to harm themselves or others. I asked them if they had ever experienced thoughts about suicide, other forms of self-harm, or about hurting their partner. Both denied any abuse, past or present.

Dan and Ellen: Personal History

Growing up, Dan learned to protect his feelings by presenting a public image that covered his lack of personal confidence. The incongruence caused by his image confused Ellen. She did not know which person was her husband; the confident and outgoing "public" Dan or the shy, withdrawn, and "depressed" husband she knew at home. Often, Ellen assumed that Dan was in a good mood, only to become frustrated when he refused to help or join a mutual activity. He often said that he did not "feel up to it," instead going off to sleep or work alone on his computer. His moods fluctuated between complacency and hopelessness. Dan admitted that he had never felt truly joyful at any time in his life.

As Ellen began speaking, Dan's posture changed. He shrunk in his chair and I clearly observed a look in his eyes that I interpreted as the essence of shame. His eyes sank, and his posture wilted in a way I had never seen before. Dan said that he felt pressured by Ellen, and this pressure caused him to "shut down." When that happened, he could not express himself or explain why talking to his wife was so difficult. He felt "safer" isolating himself rather than discussing his feelings or arguing with his wife.

Revealing Physical Abuse

Near the end of this exchange, the mood and atmosphere in the room changed. Both Dan and Ellen seemed to grow uncomfortable, almost as if they knew the time had come to reveal something that neither wanted to reveal. After a few uncomfortable moments of silence, Ellen spoke up. She said that she had physically attacked Dan on several occasions, most recently last week. This event had triggered their interest in therapy. Ellen said that she sometimes grew so frustrated by Dan's silence that she lost her "cool" and would begin slapping him about the head and face. Dan usually responded by running from the room and isolating himself even more. Sometimes, he would leave the house. Ellen claimed that she had slapped Dan on several occasions when he refused to talk. When she would calm down, Ellen would become overwhelmed with hurt and frustration caused by the physical attacks on her husband.

After this revelation, both seemed relieved that the abuse had "come out." Her physical abuse of Dan was a source of shame for both. Ellen was ashamed because she did not see herself as a violent person. Dan was ashamed because the abuse he suffered at Ellen's hand challenged his "manhood." He heard other men laughing at physically abused men, calling them "weak." Now, he was one of those "weak" men whose wife beat him up.

Questions

While there are cases of women physically abusing men, they appear rarely in the practice literature. It is less common to read about wives or female partners beating their husbands or male partners. Current law and public culture demands that practitioners and the legal system treat physical abuse seriously, especially when men are the perpetrators of violence. Since this is an unusual circumstance, but one that occurs in practice, it is important to prepare before similar cases occur in your practice.

1. Explore the domestic violence literature to learn the prevalence of women physically abusing men in relationships. What does the literature say is involved in these relationships? Why and how does this happen? Are the contexts and dynamics of these relationships similar or different from relationships where men physically abuse women? Describe the factors that contribute to women physically abusing their male partners.

2. What does the law, mandated reporter requirements, and the NASW Code of Professional Ethics (NASW, 2000) say about practitioner responsibilities in cases such as these? Are the requirements the same, or are they different?

3. Regardless of professional and legal requirements, explore your own values, attitudes, and beliefs in the context of public opinion and culture. Do these factors lead to a different handling of cases when women perpetrate domestic violence versus men?

4. How would you handle a similar situation if Dan was abusing Ellen? Discuss this issue with others in your class to help gauge culture and compare your beliefs and values. Is there a gender difference among your colleagues that affects how others would handle this issue?

Relationship History

The report of domestic violence concerned me. However, I decided to change directions for a while to learn about their relationship before the baby was born. I wanted to assess whether their reported behaviors existed from the beginning of their relationship or were new since the birth of their daughter. I also wanted to learn which patterns were characterological and which were environmental. This might play an important role in assessment and treatment planning.

Ellen and Dan had been together for three years total. They dated for eighteen months and lived together six months before marrying. At the time of our first session, they had been married one year. While they dated, Ellen said that Dan expressed himself more often and seemed to like their activities together. She also said that he seemed less intimidated by her demonstrative personality. However, she remembered times when he retreated during an argument. Ellen denied feeling frustrated during their courtship, and she certainly denied ever hitting Dan during that time. Dan also reported that their relationship was "better" during that time. He found her easier to approach and less demanding and angry.

As often happens in new relationships, it was possible that Dan and Ellen's early relationship behavior was motivated by the romantic love phase of their relationship, allowing each to overlook the other's "flaws." Ellen said that she did not notice his tendency to withdraw and Dan did not notice Ellen's tendency to get frustrated and angry. As most people have done (including most of us), it is easy to overlook so-called red flags in your partner when newly "in love." Perhaps this is what happened to Dan and Ellen. However, I was surprised that these issues did not arise during their six months of living together. Maybe it was the birth of their child after all.

Dan said that he had "always" avoided conflict, even before meeting Ellen. This ingrained pattern began long before marriage and parenthood. He stated,

> I've always hated arguing. When I was a kid, my mother would question me and pressure me into talking with her. I hated it. She always made me feel like a stupid idiot because I never gave her the right answer. I just tried to stay in my room or out with my friends as much as I could. I hate arguing, especially with someone I love.

Fighting back tears, Dan sometimes felt the same way while arguing with Ellen. With that, Dan began to cry. This was an important moment to be happening so early in our relationship. Unfortunately, our session time was ending. I found myself in a familiar dilemma; end the session or extend it to allow Dan to process his emotions. I sat in silence for a couple of minutes, and then decided to end the session. I suggested to Dan and Ellen that we continue discussing this in our next session. I complimented Dan on how well he expressed himself in front of Ellen and me, and suggested that he try doing this at home. He agreed. I thanked them both for sharing such personal and threatening information with me during our session. I then told Ellen that she needed to find other ways to vent her frustration besides attacking her husband. She nodded in agreement, and stated that she would not hit him again.

Following the session, I made a mental note to watch whether Dan routinely waited until the end of sessions to participate. Some practitioners see this as a client defense mechanism or manipulation. That is, if clients wait until the end of the session, they never have to finish what they begin, or force therapists into adapting their time schedule at the behest of their clients. I viewed it differently. Perhaps it took Dan a full session to feel safe. I began thinking about what I could do to facilitate a safe environment for Dan to express himself earlier.

While I had worked with cases involving domestic violence, this was my first case where the female was the abuser and the male the victim. I was unsure how to approach the subject in session. During the session, I tried to discover if the abuse needed immediate intervention, or if the risk was low enough for us to handle it as part of ongoing therapy. Based on Ellen's response to my direct approach, I did not believe that Dan was significantly at-risk. I also believed that Ellen could control herself, now that her secret was out. Therefore, I told Ellen that she needed to cease, in hopes that her attacks would stop before escalating into abuse that was more serious. At that point, I hoped for the best but planned to query the couple about it in every session thereafter.

Questions

1. Building on your investigation and exploration of this topic earlier, how should the author have addressed this issue? Develop and defend your opinion of her comments and actions with Dan and Ellen.

2. If Dan was the perpetrator and Ellen the victim; would you have expected the author to handle it differently? How and why? Thoroughly defend your position and debate this subject in class with student-colleagues.

Dan and Ellen: Family History

When Dan and Ellen returned, I asked about their week, and checked to see that they did not have any crises. While they both agreed that little had changed, Ellen proudly stated that she had not "blown up" at Dan when he went to his room. This verified to me that she could control her abusive behavior and that Dan was not at-risk for further victimization.

I asked if we could spend this session discussing their family histories. I wanted to learn about any associations between their family-of-origins and their marriage. Commonly, couples project or superimpose assumptions based on child/parent relationships onto adult partners. For example, Luguet (1996) suggests that intense negative feelings, unrealistic expectations, fearing abuse or rejection, and assuming to know what partners are thinking or feeling are all common distortions that move from family-of-origins to adult relationships.

While I had little information to go on, I assumed that Dan and Ellen were playing out childhood conflicts with each other, and that these conflicts intensified when they became parents. Discussing their family histories would either confirm or refute this assumption. If they were repeating old behavioral patterns, I hoped that discussing their family histories would help each understand how old issues and patterns affected their lives in the present.

Ellen's Family-of-Origin

Ellen grew up, along with her younger brother and sister, in a "traditional" family setting. Her mother took care of the home while her father worked long days, came home, ate, watched television, and slept. She said that he was a "drinker," who often became "nasty" when he was drunk. Her definition of "nasty" included verbal abuse of her mother, yelling at the kids, and sometimes physically acting-out. When he became angry, her father would slam and break things around the house and garage. She did not recall ever seeing him hit her mother, but he did spank the kids occasionally. She said that spanking was not abuse, but proper parental discipline.

Her mother was a passive woman who spent her life trying to keep the family peaceful and her husband relaxed and satisfied. Her job was to make his life as easy as possible, by sheltering him from problems with the kids, and making sure that everyone was quiet at night so he could rest. This family description is consistent for families with a chemically dependent parent (Johnson, 2004).

From her childhood experience, Ellen learned to be the "perfect" wife and mother. That is, she learned that the woman's job was to raise the kids and keep the home calm for her husband. She also learned that women did not argue or confront their husbands. They remained quiet and nice. Ellen openly resented this role and vowed never to be like her mother. She frequently expressed her feelings to Dan and expected him to participate in the family equally. Hence, Ellen provided a striking contrast to her mother, who always hid her resentment and rarely placed demands on her husband. According to Ellen, since she worked outside the home, she believed that she deserved Dan's support around the house and with the baby. Besides her willingness to verbalize her disappointment with the marriage, Ellen also exhibited several controlling behaviors that she learned from her father.

For example, Ellen said that she could not "let arguments go." She watched her father instigate arguments with her mother and harass her until she cried. Ellen often did the same thing with Dan. While Ellen achieved her childhood goal of not marrying someone like her father, in many ways, she assumed her father's role in her marriage. When Dan refused to finish an argument, Ellen could not "leave it alone." She would repeatedly demand that Dan continue talking with her until they found a resolution. Ellen stated (and Dan agreed) that once she became angry, they had little chance of finding a satisfactory resolution to their argument, but she persisted anyhow. When the pattern escalated, she lost her temper and struck Dan.

In many ways, Ellen married someone like her mother. Similar to her mother, Dan also had difficulty expressing his thoughts and feelings. Other times, he simply refused to try. The more Ellen pressed for dialogue, the more silent Dan became. The more silent Dan became, the more Ellen pressed him for dialogue, and so on. I asked Ellen if her pattern with Dan was similar to her parents. She sat silently for a few moments. Then, with a look of realization, she agreed with my assessment. For the first time, it appeared that Ellen identified the ironic role reversal in her marriage. While this did not mean she would change, I saw it as a good first step.

Dan's Family-of-Origin

Dan grew up as the youngest of four siblings. He described his parents as "neglectful" people who "never supported" him or his siblings. His father was a businessperson that worked long hours. He never had time for the children. Dan said that his father was difficult to please, so he stopped trying. Dan's mother also worked outside the home, and rarely paid attention to him.

His parents always seemed too busy for him and his siblings. Dan grew up believing that he could not do anything well enough to please his father or his mother. He said they never told him that they loved him, nor could he remember hugging his parents. According to Dan, his family did not exhibit healthy, open communication about anything, especially their emotions.

To cope, Dan retreated to his bedroom or into sports, learning to turn his anger and fear inward until "blowing up" in an angry outburst. He further claimed that each of his siblings have personal troubles too. Each had been married and divorced, and his two sisters were "regulars" in therapist's offices. While he was not sure about the nature of their problems, he did say that each had problems because of how they were treated as children.

Dan believed that his family life was "different" from other families. Other parents attended ballgames and loved their children. His did not. Dan felt distant from his parents because they never asked about his life or had a decent conversation. He was never touched kindly and he never felt "good enough." His mother would occasionally tell him that he was a "good kid" but "she didn't know me, so it didn't matter what she said." Because of his distant and impersonal familial relationships, Dan did not have anyone to talk with, so he kept his feelings inside. He said that he had "no idea" what it meant to be loved, or love in a family context.

When I asked Dan what he needed from his parents, he replied,

> The same thing I need from Ellen—someone to hug me, tell me they love me, be there, teach me, someone interested in who I am.

I asked Ellen if she wanted to respond to Dan. At first, she spoke directly to me. I gently redirected her attention toward Dan and asked her to speak to him. Ellen slid herself toward him on the couch, took his hand and said,

> I do love you and I want you to know how much this marriage means to me and how much you mean to me. I want to be with you, but I also need conversation and communication. I want to know you, but you make it very hard for me.

Dan sat silently. I could see that he wanted to respond but he did not feel safe sharing his feelings with her. After a long silence, I prematurely jumped in. Just as I began to speak, Dan spoke up.

> I know you love me. Sometimes it is just so hard to believe it. I want to tell you my feelings but it's like, they are stuck somewhere. I get confused and can't think clear. I worry I'll say the wrong thing or it will come out stupid. You know how I hate to be embarrassed.

This time, I allowed this exchange to sink in. Our session was ending, so I asked Dan if it was important for Ellen to approve of him. With some effort, he said that it was the most important thing in his life, and that he thought by telling her how he felt; she would disapprove and leave him. We ended the session with this powerful insight. I hoped that by clarifying the deep-rooted hold their dysfunctional childhoods had on them, that each would see how they projected onto each other the role their parents had played.

Ellen and Dan as Individuals

After discussing their families and marriage, I looked at the behaviors and symptoms each presented during our first two sessions. I had a hunch that Dan might have some form of depression, but was unsure about Ellen. Before proceeding to treatment and intervention planning, I needed to examine each individually to ensure that we had a proper diagnosis, if any, and therefore, an appropriate treatment and intervention plan.

Dan

I asked Dan to take a depression screening tool based on the Beck Depression Scale, other well-known depression screening instruments, and various criteria in the DSM-IV-TR (APA, 2000). On this particular instrument, it took an affirmative answer to five or more questions to indicate possible depression. Dan answered affirmatively to eleven of the twelve questions asked; clearly indicating that he needed further assessment for depression. Ellen believed that Dan exhibited all twelve symptoms. As I examined the various criteria in the DSM-IV-TR, there were three possibilities. Dan fit the criteria for Major Depressive Disorder, Dysthymic Disorder, or both.

Dan described himself as feeling depressed most of his life. Ellen's account supported Dan's perception. He occasionally overate for comfort, had low energy, slept a lot, had low self-esteem, struggled to concentrate, could not make decisions, and frequently felt hopeless about his life. Dan said that he struggled with these symptoms most of his life, but they had intensified during the past year.

Dan diligently tried to exhibit a positive appearance but usually toward session's end, he would deflate and his mood became hollow and sad. Part of Ellen's frustration was her belief that Dan behaved differently at work. Therefore, she believed that he could control himself but chose not to. She was unaware of Dan's need for external approval. At home, he relaxed and let his "guard" down. Ellen often was the only person who saw the "real" Dan, and she did not understand him.

Dan did report having a "few" friends at work that he talked to during the day. He also enjoyed his softball teammates. However, he said that he had never been someone with many friends. He liked to keep his friendships "at arms length" and out of his personal life.

Ellen

Ellen reported occasional feelings of depression. However, her feelings of agitation and guilt, along with periods of sleeplessness and depressed mood were different from Dan's. Ellen reported that these feelings began only after the baby was born and were a direct result of her interactions with Dan. That is, Ellen did not report symptoms on a daily basis, nor did she experience these symptoms prior to her marriage and childbirth. I remained concerned about her tendency to attack Dan physically out of frustration. She reported that her frustration and anger toward Dan built to the point of "explosion," and that during these times she simply could not stop herself from hitting him.

Since the birth of their child and her changed schedule at work, Ellen reported fewer opportunities to interact outside the home. She had few friends "left" after the last year, and could not find time to see what few friends she had left in her life. Since the baby was born, she reported little outside activity, feeling isolated in her home and marriage. Prior to her marriage, Ellen said that she was a social woman, with many friends and outside interests. These had all slipped away over the past two years.

Questions

Now that the author has presented Dan and Ellen's personal histories and before reading her assessment and diagnoses below, perform the following exercises based on your education, experience, the professional literature, and best practice evidence. To increase the learning potential of this exercise, you may want to do this in a small group with other students.

1. Based on the information contained above, construct a three-generation genogram and eco-map that represent Dan and Ellen's personal, familial, and environmental circumstances. What further information do you need to complete this exercise? What patterns do these two important graphical assessment tools demonstrate?

2. Develop a list of Dan, Ellen, and the couple's problems and strengths.

3. Write a three-page narrative assessment that encompasses Dan and Ellen's multi-systemic issues and strengths. Review Chapter 1, if needed. This narrative should provide a comprehensive and multi-systemic explanation of their life as they prepare to undergo therapy with the author.

4. Try to identify the theoretical model or approach that you used to guide your assessment. According to the literature, what other theoretical options are available and how would these change the nature of your assessment?

5. End by developing multi-axial DSM-IV-TR diagnoses for both Dan and Ellen. Be sure to look for evidence of multiple diagnoses on Axis I. Provide the list of client symptoms that you used to justify your diagnostic decisions. What, if any, information was missing that would make this an easier task?

Multi-Systemic Assessment

Based on the information described above, I looked at two primary areas needing attention: (1) Dan and Ellen's potential mental health diagnoses, and (2) the problems in their marriage that included Dan's withdrawal from Ellen and Ellen's reaction to his behavior. Both areas interacted to create the multi-systemic case context that I worked with during my time with this couple.

Dan's Diagnosis

I believed that Dan fit the DSM-IV-TR (APA, 2000) criteria for Dysthymic Disorder, early onset. Dysthymia is a chronic form of depression lasting at least two years in adults and one year in children. It differs from Major Depression in that it is usually less disabling, but more chronic. People with Dysthymic Disorder often work, maintain their hobbies, and present a balanced outward appearance. The disruption in life usually occurs internally through health problems or externally through troubled and disrupted personal relationships. At the time of our assessment, I believed that this description fit Dan perfectly.

Ellen's Diagnosis

I did not believe that Ellen fit the criteria for any of the classified mood or anxiety disorders. It appeared to me that her symptoms were environmentally triggered and not pervasive enough to warrant a specific mental health diagnosis. However, she did have problems. Most notably, Ellen had become isolated from her world since childbirth and lacked a social support network. This led to her inability to process anger and frustration appropriately, setting the stage for her violent "blow-ups" and physical abuse of her husband. Her family had become too central in her life. She had no vehicle for taking time away for herself.

Marital Problems

Dan and Ellen's marriage was troubled. While they reported no problems prior to the birth of their child, there was evidence that the problems had already begun. Ellen was a forthright and assertive woman, determined not to assume the role her mother fulfilled in her family-of-origin. That is, she was not going to be the "perfect" wife, living only to support, nurture, and be subservient to her husband. She was willing to "call" Dan on behavior she disapproved of and insist that Dan participate as an equal functioning member of their young family.

Dan was the opposite. While he craved public respect and approval, he was a chronically depressed man who feared conflict and confrontation. He was unable to engage with Ellen in discussion about their problems, and found himself unable to discuss his feelings at any time. Instead, Dan retreated to his bedroom, computer station, work, or softball games. What Ellen defined as withholding behavior, Dan saw as self-protection. Growing up in his family, Dan never learned to interact openly and forthrightly in a family. He feared intimacy, mainly because he was afraid of being "exposed" as the unlovable person he believed that he was. In other words, Dan had lived his whole life grappling with a sense of shame, demonstrated by his need to present an upbeat and confident public image along with his inability to deal with Ellen as a human being with feelings.

Parenthood seemed to be the trigger issue for the cyclical behavior pattern that consumed, and nearly wrecked, their marriage. Both partners were living out childhood scripts with the other, in an effort to rectify issues from their families-of-origin. Because of her disrespect for her mother, Ellen assumed the leadership role in her family, similar to her father. On the other hand, Dan tried proving himself as a lovable, competent, and successful man, reversing his overwhelming sense of shame that began in childhood. When these two scripts collided, they began a family "dance" that ultimately led to withdrawal, frustration, anger, and occasional violent outbursts.

Questions

Before moving on, compare the assessment and diagnostic statement you developed to the author's. Where do you find points of agreement and disagreement? Discuss these issues with student-colleagues and use the professional literature to analyze the differences.

1. What implications for treatment surfaced because of differences in assessment and diagnoses?

2. Explain these differences as part of a treatment plan. That is, develop a treatment plan for Dan and Ellen from your assessment. Include the type of treatment, theoretical model, or approach (approaches) you would use, and how these differ from the author.

Treatment Planning

During our next session, Dan, Ellen, and I developed a treatment plan to address the issues discussed above. The plan had two significant elements: (1) refer Dan to a medical practitioner for confirming diagnosis and potential medication, and (2) marital and individual therapy for each to address the various personal and relationship problems.

Goal one would be addressed by their family doctor. I proposed the following plan to address goal two:

1. Imago Therapy to address communication problems in their marriage.
2. Cognitive-behavioral therapy to address Dan and Ellen's distorted thinking patterns.
3. Cognitive-behavioral therapy aimed at resolving Dan's overwhelming sense of personal shame and guilt.
4. Motivate Ellen to find and use outside social support networks of friends and coworkers.

Questions

1. **Compare the treatment plan you established above with the author's treatment plan. What differences and similarities exist between the plans? How do you account for the differences? Use the professional literature and practice evidence to analyze both plans, and the differences between them.**

2. **Develop a revised treatment plan based on information provided by the author, your original plan, and the practice literature. What does the evidenced-based practice literature say are the most effective ways to treat clients with Dan and Ellen's problems and strengths? Using the rationale from the literature and your experience, develop a position on this issue.**

Course of Treatment

Engaging Clients about Medication

During our next session, I explained Dysthymic Disorder and its implications to Dan and Ellen. Dan seemed surprised by this, while Ellen agreed. I explained that many see depression as the "common cold" of mental disorders. At least one out of every ten Americans experience depression or manic-depressive illness at some point in their lifetime. This amounts to ten million women and five million men currently suffering from a form of depression (APA, 2000). Yet, only one-third of people with depressive illness ever get diagnosed and properly treated. Depression accounts for the greatest number of days lost from work, often because it is accompanied by physical illness (DePaulo, 2002).

I also discussed the possibility of medication management. I explained that a combination of medication and psychotherapy provided the best way to treat Dan's moderate to severe depressive illness. I provided Dan and Ellen with educational materials that demonstrated the efficacy of medication and psychotherapy as a treatment for depression, hoping that Dan would agree to meet his doctor about this possibility.

As is often the case, Dan was unwilling to use prescription medication. However, he was willing to take St. John's Wort at his wife's suggestion. Since many believe that St. John's Wort is an effective remedy for mild to moderate depressive symptoms, I supported this idea. His reaction to this herbal remedy might offer clues about whether Dan's depression was biochemical or caused by maladaptive relationship skills. If his depressive symptoms were environmental, St. John's Wort would not provide relief. He would only benefit from it if he had a biochemical imbalance.

Since it is an herbal remedy, St. John's Wort does not require a medical prescription. However, I insisted that Dan talk to his doctor before taking it to ensure that there were no potentially harmful side effects. I hoped that his physician would convince him to try prescription medication if the herbal remedy did not work. I have several clients who found symptom relief with St. John's Wort, with no obvious side effects. Therefore, I felt comfortable supporting their decision as long as Dan consulted his doctor. He agreed.

With the resurgence of natural, homeopathic remedies, I have developed a more holistic approach to therapy. Knowing about alternative treatments (such as herbal remedies, massage, acupuncture, or activities such as yoga) allows me to offer alternatives to clients that others avoid. However, any suggestion of alternative treatment requires a thorough client history and doctor's approval, or bad things can happen. A colleague once suggested racquetball as exercise without realizing that the client previously had knee surgery. The client injured her knee while playing, and my colleague felt awful about it.

Fortunately, by the fifth week of taking St. John's Wort, Dan reported feeling less depressed and no side effects. He could control his temper, felt less defensive, expressed himself better, and felt happier. Simultaneously, Dan began understanding his depressive symptoms better. Hence, he continued taking St. John's Wort. His improvement thrilled and relieved Ellen. She said that Dan was less irritable and moody, withdrew less, and was more positive and communicative.

Imago Therapy

Given Dan's improvements, we began using Imago Therapy (Luguet, 1996) to strengthen their relationship. Imago therapy requires practitioners to take an active role in helping clients discover and understand how attitudes and patterns shaped during childhood repeat in adult relationships. They agreed to an eight-session format.

Imago therapy works well for people motivated to seek help, and the practitioner's main task is to provide an atmosphere where clients can understand their attitudes, clarify their feelings, and learn to accept others and themselves. This treatment approach focuses on helping couples to recognize how their deficits complimented each other and initially attracted them to each other.

During Dan and Ellen's first Imago Therapy session, they focused on identifying their role patterns, or their family "dance," and how this pattern affected their marriage. We identified that Dan's passive approach at home had given Ellen the freedom to run the household as she pleased. This pattern served both well, until their daughter was born. The added responsibility of parenthood overwhelmed Ellen and she began to grow resentful because Dan did not help her. Dan initially responded to Ellen's growing criticism with a quiet, resentful compliance. However, he, too, became overwhelmed. With that, he withdrew into the basement to work on his computer or to bed.

Imago Therapy works by teaching a form of communication called "couple's dialogue" (Luguet, 1996). Couples listen attentively to each other and repeat the exact words they had just heard spoken. Listeners cannot formulate a defense or a comeback. Their focus must be on hearing what their partner said. The talker speaks in short sentences, and the listener repeats back what they heard by saying, "What I heard you say is . . ." or "If I got this right, you said. . . ." When the first speaker finishes, the roles reverse. This intervention works because it focuses on minimizing accusations and defensiveness, while reinforcing empathy and compassion.

Dan felt safe using couple's dialogue to communicate with Ellen during therapy. They shared many heartfelt moments that drew them closer and renewed their sense of hopefulness. However, at home things were different. They had trouble transferring skills learned in therapy to their home. For example, at home when they began arguing, Ellen often asked for couple's dialogue. Instead of participating, Dan became "jumbled inside," had difficulty listening and formulating words, and believed Ellen was "out to get him." He would then become angry and withdraw for hours.

To help Dan, I decided that he should imagine a sign around Ellen's neck that said *Not Mom* in an effort to resist childhood triggers. Ellen would reinforce this message by stating, "I'm your wife, not your mom," in a loving tone. The implication was that she loved him, saw his worth and value. This would only work if Ellen said her line in a loving way. I worried that Ellen, because she was usually straightforward and sometimes harsh in her vocal tones, might respond to Dan in an angry and sarcastic tone, evoking his shame. I worked with Ellen on the quality of her response and with Dan on ways to deal with Ellen if she became sarcastic. If that happened, we decided that Dan could use couple's dialogue to express how he felt. He refused, claiming that this would be too overwhelming. While we did not solve this problem, I acknowledged that they had taken positive steps and were moving toward success.

During the remainder of their Imago Therapy, Dan continued having difficulty expressing himself, while Ellen grew increasingly frustrated. However, Ellen's frustration was different from before. She now understood that Dan was struggling with a real problem and not withdrawing just to make her angry. This allowed me to relax about the possibility of physical abuse, but I still asked about it each week to make sure.

As time passed, Dan began appearing more withdrawn than before. Ellen could not explain his downturn because they were getting along better, having fewer arguments, and more moments of intimacy. Dan could not explain it either. Perhaps the St. John's Wort was not working. Dan insisted that it was working fine, again refusing to see his doctor about medication. I backed off.

I was debating whether this was an appropriate time to bring Dan's vulnerability into our sessions. His behavior reflected growing anxiety as he tried to express his thoughts and feelings, often a clue that clients feel vulnerable. I decided that pushing this issue might reinforce his defense system because, when feeling threatened, Dan wanted to hide his shame by projecting a confident appearance, or withdrawing from the encounter. He was not ready for this yet.

Instead, I chose to focus on his strengths. I pointed out how Dan's emotional expressiveness had improved his relationship with Ellen. I told Dan that I appreciated the risks he was taking and understood how difficult this was for him, but that he was moving in a positive direction. I could sense his commitment to undoing the damage of his childhood by replacing his perceptions with healthier, more productive skills.

While I was talking, I could see Dan sit up with pride. He and Ellen smiled at each other. It was clear that this couple needed hope. When they entered therapy, they were doubtful about whether their marriage could survive. While we were a long way from definitively answering that question, unless they discovered a sense of hope, it would never work out for them. As a colleague of mine once said, if all he accomplishes in one hour of therapy is to provide a sense of hope, then he had a good session. I agree.

Questions

The author just finished discussing a model for relationship therapy called Imago Therapy, which relies on structured communication techniques to help couples learn to communicate directly and honestly. The practice literature is filled with various models and approaches for relationship therapy.

1. Explore the practice literature to find other similar or different approaches to relationship therapy that you think might be effective with Dan and Ellen. Describe them, highlighting their theoretical foundations, how problems are defined, the role of the practitioner, and suggested interventions.

2. Based on the information in this case, decide what model or approach described above you would use if you were the practitioner responsible for Dan and Ellen's case. Defend your decision from the practice literature, best practice evidence, your experience, and/or through discussion with student-colleagues.

3. Critique the approach used by the author in this case. What are the strengths and weaknesses of this model, and decide whether you agree with the author's choice of intervention.

Cognitive-Behavioral Model

I began meeting with Dan during Imago Therapy to work on his thinking patterns and shame with a cognitive-behavioral treatment approach. However, before moving into this discussion, I include a brief discussion of shame and the power it has in people's lives.

Shame

Shame is a powerful emotion that begins in early childhood and manifests throughout the life cycle. Shame is associated with self-doubt and self-blame, and refers to core aspects of a person's persona. Shame is the overwhelming feeling that occurs when people believe they are bad. It differs from guilt. Guilt occurs when people believe they have done something bad. Therefore, guilt is driven by behaviors in context, while shame becomes people's primary, ongoing feeling about themselves as people. Shame reflects on a person's sense of self, well-being, and self-efficacy. Guilt is usually a short-term emotion that hinges on certain events or behaviors in a person's life.

Young children rely on their parents, close relatives, peers, and teachers to help develop their personal identity. When parents reassure and affirm their child's worth through positive feelings and behaviors, children develop a sense of security about their worth as unique individuals. These children believe that they are lovable because they were treated as lovable people. Because they believe they are worthwhile, these children often feel safe letting other's see their "real" self.

When children grow up with anger, expressions of irritability, disgust, or silence, they incorporate into their identity a sense of ambivalence, anxiety, and distrust of their value and worth as human beings. A depleted sense of well-being shapes their essential self, and children who blame themselves for the negative reaction they receive from others often begin believing that there is something wrong with them (Kaufman, 1992). Without external proof that their negative thoughts are invalid, these children believe they are bad, worthless, and unlovable people. Hence, they begin a self-defeating cycle that often becomes a self-fulfilling prophecy.

If not addressed, a shame-based approach to life persists into adulthood. Anyone who does not receive external support to help counterbalance shame develops a shame-based identity. Shame disrupts the process of healthy character development and clouds people's lives and relationships. Often, these individuals put most of their efforts into proving their worth, or presenting a public image that covers their profound sense of shame. This was how I saw Dan as we began individual therapy.

Dan's Individual Therapy

Dan and I established three primary goals for individual therapy: (1) Dan would experience himself as less vulnerable, more congruent, and with increased self-regard; (2) Dan would demonstrate signs of improved self-esteem by communicating more openly about his real self, and (3) Dan would exhibit less shame and anxiety as demonstrated by fewer introverted and inhibited behaviors.

It took several individual sessions before I understood how significant shame was as an issue for Dan. His overwhelming desire to avoid his sense of shame by having others see him as competent motivated Dan to present himself differently outside the family than he did at home. He began each session with me bright, confident, and engaging. However, as time passed, Dan's appearance shifted from confident to uneasy, and from hopeful to sad. It became apparent how insecure and vulnerable he was; something Dan desperately wanted to hide.

The dynamic of incongruence between his appearance and his feelings made Ellen wonder if she ever really "knew" Dan before they were married. It was clear that his self-perception differed from his public persona. Dan approached the world from a position grounded in personal shame, leading him to hide his "real" self, causing significant social and personal maladjustment (Turner, 1996).

As stated earlier, I approached Dan's shame with a cognitive-behavioral approach. Cognitive-behavioral therapy hypothesizes that people's thoughts influence their emotions and behaviors. Cognitive-behavioral therapy is goal-oriented and problem-focused. It aims to teach the client to be self-sufficient in managing his or her thoughts, feelings, and behaviors. The practitioner plays an active role in helping clients recognize distorted thinking patterns and foster new, more productive thoughts to replace the distorted thinking. The primary treatment goal is to help recognize people's automatic, negative thoughts and to reframe them in a way that allows for behavior change (Beck, 1995).

Dan was unaware that his brain processed automatic thoughts or that he had ongoing, internal dialogue about his feelings and behaviors. When he recognized his highly negative, self-critical thoughts, he was surprised. He was unaware of the influence his negative thoughts had on his mood, self-esteem, and behavior, especially toward Ellen. I worked with Dan to track his internal self-talk and find ways to change it from negative to positive. He began tracking perceptions of himself in relation to others more effectively. This led to more in-depth discussions about his life, perceptions, and his family-of-origin.

As Dan became aware of his family-of-origin issues, he recognized that he responded most negatively to his mother. Dan believed that his mother was "insecure, simple, and scared"; someone who refused to discuss issues and would lie to him on the rare occasions when Dan confronted her behavior. In her own way, Dan said that his mother was a "my way or the highway" type of person. She controlled the family, and Dan realized that his father was powerless in his marriage. Dan resented her.

He also realized that Ellen shared many of her traits, and that he felt as powerless around his wife as his father did around his mother. As it turned out, Dan was angry with his mother, father, Ellen, and himself. He also realized that his anger played a significant role in his marital problems and fed his depression. Dan was making progress, but it was a long, uphill climb for him.

Over the next few sessions, our work seemed to be paying off. Dan began reporting that "things" were going "great." Ellen and he only had one small argument, which Dan said he had handled "maturely." Dan had intended to work late and Ellen thought he was coming home early. She called his office to see where he was and when he told her that he needed to stay late, she got angry and began to criticize him, triggering his shame and anger. She had asked him to come home before her bedtime at 11:00 p.m.

Dan initially became frustrated because he had work to do, and he felt that she was being demanding and controlling. He noticed himself becoming irritable and short-tempered. He recognized this pattern, rethought his perspective, and settled himself down. He came home by 11:00 that evening and they talked about the incident. Dan said that he felt better after they talked and was proud of his progress.

He accomplished this because of how he interpreted Ellen's behavior. When his depression was under control, he did not think of Ellen's behavior as controlling or judgmental. In the most recent incident, he understood her disappointment and did not interpret her as a controlling person. He learned to list his negative thoughts and the positive responses needed to manage his thoughts and behaviors. He recognized how his negative, depressed thoughts triggered inappropriate responses. For example:

Trigger: There she goes telling me what to do again.

Positive Response: She's not my mom.

Trigger: There's one rule for her and one for me.

Positive Response: It's not that way, we're equal.

Trigger: Everything has to be her way.

Positive Response: We're more equal than that; it's not her way all the time.

Trigger: You don't understand me or what I'm going through.

Positive Response: If I explain it to her, she will be able to understand.

Trigger: It's always my fault, you're always right.

Positive Response: We're both right and wrong.

Trigger: You're not going to tell me what to do.

Positive Response: She's not my mom.

Dan responded well to this approach because it provided a structured plan that he could practice at home. Our "dress rehearsals" helped him to respond appropriately during moments of stress. Without this technique, he resorted to his "old way" of thinking and suffered negative consequences. He had progressed to the point that he appreciated the benefits of "talking things out" with Ellen rather than withdrawing. His ability to see issues from her perspective reduced his anger. Hence, he could remain calm and monitor his feelings. He used the phrase "time out" to remind himself to stop and think before reacting impulsively.

I also taught Dan to rate his anxiety on a ten-point Likert scale, with "one" representing "no anxiety" and "ten" the worst possible anxiety. As Dan began self-rating his anxiety, he recognized how his anxiety could escalate and overwhelm him. Our goal was to have Dan recognize, by using his scale on a daily basis, his escalating anxiety before he became overwhelmed and shut-down. Dan decided that his shut-down point was a "six or seven." He said that if we had rated his anxiety one year earlier, it would have been a "two or three" on his scale. Dan was beginning to take control of his life, symptoms, and moods by implementing several self-help strategies before losing control.

With continued practice and increased awareness, Dan could slow himself down and not overreact to Ellen at home. Once he recognized how his childhood influenced his behavior and that Ellen was "not out to get him," he could alter his levels of shame and anxiety. Once his thoughts and feelings became more positive, his behavior followed. I often tell clients that change comes in three steps. First, they must decide what behavior they want to change. Second, they decide what they want instead. Third, they must practice their new behavior. Dan did just that for several months, and found success.

Questions

The author used a cognitive-behavioral approach to work with Dan, and it seemed successful to this point. Similar to the relationship therapy discussed earlier, the practice literature is filled with individual approaches that could be employed with Dan.

1. Explore the practice literature to find other similar or different approaches to relationship therapy that you think might be effective with Dan and Ellen. Describe them, highlighting their theoretical foundations, how problems are defined, the role of the practitioner, and suggested interventions.

2. Based on the information in this case, decide what model or approach described above you would use if you were the practitioner responsible for Dan and Ellen's case. Defend your decision from the practice literature, best practice evidence, your experience, and/or through discussion with student-colleagues.

3. Critique the approach used by the author in this case. What are the strengths and weaknesses of this model, and decide whether you agree with the author's choice of intervention.

Dealing with Dan's Depression

Dan and his wife continued in marital therapy after completing Imago Therapy. We continued to use cognitive-behavioral techniques to help Dan manage his moods, avoid overreacting, and build a positive self-concept. He and Ellen still struggled to communicate, so they kept using couple's dialogue to express their feelings and locate solutions. Approximately six months into treatment, it became apparent that the St. John's Wort was not sufficiently managing Dan's depressive symptoms. Perhaps it was time for medication.

Medication Management

When a client presents with an apparent biochemical depression, my job is to prepare them for a possible treatment regimen that includes medication. This is often not easy for clients to accept. At the very least, it intimidates them. Therefore, my job is to engage clients successfully around the notion that medication might be helpful. For example, I often encourage clients to talk with their physician about the possibility of taking medication to help manage their symptoms. I let them know that if their brain chemistry is out of balance, no talk therapy or positive thinking in the world was going to relieve their symptoms. In fact, untreated biological depression can prevent clients from feeling better no matter how hard they work to overcome it.

Science has yet to determine why the brain's neurotransmitters malfunction in some people and not others (Ginsberg, Nackerud, & Larrison, 2004). However, scientists believe that antidepressants are an effective way to manage psychological illness, not cure the illness. I told Dan that medication would help ease his symptoms so that he could effectively work toward solving his problems. Depression is serious. One bout of depression correlates with a 50 percent chance of having a second. After two bouts, the possibility of having a third is 70 percent. After three episodes, there is a 90 percent chance of a fourth occurrence (Tolman, 2001).

After agreeing to see his doctor, and with their written permission, I faxed Dan's physician a letter that reads as follows:

> Dear Dr. Bruce,
>
> Dan and his wife Ellen came to see me for marital counseling from July through January. They have worked hard to create a strong marriage and are a delightful couple.
>
> Dan was struggling with symptoms of depression at the start of therapy. He chose to try St. John's Wort and had some benefit on 1200 mg. However, his depres-

sion worsened and he missed work yesterday due to feeling overwhelmed and being unable to get out of bed.

My guess is he would benefit from a prescription antidepressant rather than an herbal remedy to treat his worsening symptoms. They plan to continue in therapy with me so I will help monitor his progress. I look forward to your recommendation regarding his treatment. If you have any questions, please contact me.

Dan went to see his doctor, who prescribed a popular antidepressant medication. After some initial start-up relief, this medication also stopped working. Dr. Bruce doubled the daily dosage. Once again, Dan initially experienced improvement in his mood but also experienced sexual dysfunction, a common side effect. Fortunately, this side effect remitted about two weeks later. I let Dan know that he should discuss his concerns with his prescribing physician.

Education is an important social worker function in medication management. When clients do not know what to expect from medication, they often do not comply. Anxious clients are often too afraid to begin taking medication for fear of a bad reaction. At other times, anxious clients overreact to minor side effects. Depressed clients often see the situation through a negative frame of reference and view taking medication as a statement of failure or weakness and, therefore, resist compliance.

At first, Dan complied with his medication regimen. However, after a few weeks Dan's depression returned. Dan's doctor prescribed a second antidepressant to add to the original antidepressant. Doctors may combine antidepressant medications when a client does not respond to the initial intervention.

Social Work Role in Medication Management

I believe that social work practitioners must keep abreast of advancements in the field of psychopharmacology when treating mental health issues. However, while it is important to understand therapeutic medications, there are differences of opinion in the field about what role practitioners should play in medication management. Much of the field believes that medication and medication management is the purview of the medical profession (i.e., psychiatrist, doctors, physician assistants and nurses), and that social workers should stay out of it. Others, such as me, believe otherwise.

I recently attended a conference on depression presented by a MSW-level practitioner. The presenter discussed the importance of medication as an adjunct to outpatient therapy. She added that social workers have professional boundaries pertaining to medication. That is, social workers must not suggest particular medications or discuss the specifics of medications with clients. She detailed the inherent legal dangers that nonmedical professionals face if they overstep the boundaries of their profession.

During my nineteen years of work, I have developed a specialty in treating biochemically depressed and anxious clients. I spent the first twelve years of my professional career working with two psychiatrists, who taught me about the medical side of treatment. I monitored client responses to medication, notifying the psychiatrist if their clients experienced side effects or were noncompliant. They also expected that if I identified a client who appeared to be suffering from a biochemical imbalance that I refer him or her for medical treatment.

Hence, I came to recognize potential biochemical imbalances and learned to coordinate treatment with the psychiatrist and/or the primary care physician. I learned that my involvement helped clients improve their medication compliance and overall therapeutic outcome. This role is vital in mental health treatment when medication is required. Since we (social workers/practitioners) see clients more frequently than physicians do, we can monitor their behavior, the effects of medication, and work closely with clients and physicians to ensure proper care.

Yet, I am not a doctor. Therefore, because of professional boundaries, I am cautious about how I approach doctors and clients about medication. Physicians often consider my observations when reviewing their client's medication needs. These clients benefit from having me function as an advocate with their physician. I am always clear with clients that their medical professional, and not me, will make all the decisions regarding their medication. I explain that as a social worker, I cannot prescribe medication or advise them. However, I do educate clients to help them communicate more effectively with their physicians. Many clients feel intimidated by their physician and indicate that they are doing fine, when they actually have notable side effects or limited benefit.

Therefore, I encourage every social work practitioner to develop relationships with psychiatrists. Primary care physicians are capable of handling "easy to treat" psychiatric cases, but generally welcome a referral to a qualified psychiatrist for the more difficult to treat cases. Primary care physicians are often thankful when social workers make referrals, send introductory letters to psychiatrists, and support client compliance with medical recommendations. By providing this function, treatment outcomes likely improve, benefiting clients, practitioners, and primary care physicians.

Moreover, it is important that the psychiatrist respects and values your role with clients; not all psychiatrists do. Dr. Farr (whom I refer to later) is the only psychiatrist in my nineteen-year career that sends me progress notes on clients I refer to him. Over time, I became comfortable calling him for support with difficult to treat clients.

Psychotropic medication has become standard treatment for many mental disorders (Evans & Sullivan, 2001). Psychiatrists who once conducted traditional psychotherapy sessions are now primarily medication managers. When follow-up appointments with physicians are not scheduled for one to three months duration, it is important that the therapist observe the client's response to medications because of their influence on outpatient treatment goals and outcomes. Because of the preeminence of medication in mental health treatment, social workers and other nonmedical helping professionals must become knowledgeable and comfortable working with medicated and medically supervised clients. This is current state-of-the-art in mental health treatment.

Questions

In the preceding discussion, the author suggested a controversial level of involvement in medication management. Many social workers believe that a firm boundary between the medical and social work profession is mandatory. Social workers have no business becoming involved in a client's medication regimen, beyond a monitoring or advocacy function. The author calls for a more professionally involved role.

1. Review the Code of Professional Ethics (NASW, 2000) and locate any standards that apply to this issue. Also, read the professional practice literature regarding best practice methods as it relates to the profession's involvement with medical professionals. Accordingly, present evidence on both sides of this issue. What is the consensus of the social work profession as it relates to this topic?

2. Based on your research and experience, formulate your professional position on the issue. How will/do you operate in your practice career when it pertains to client medication? Do you agree or disagree with the author's position? Defend your position.

Dan's Ongoing Treatment

After establishing himself on antidepressant medication, Dan and I continued working to improve his self-concept, reduce his shame, and manage his negative self-talk. He wanted to perceive himself as a valuable, worthwhile human being, leading him to become more confident and less vulnerable to Ellen's criticisms. He also wanted to communicate more freely with Ellen, especially when they disagreed. His desire to set his own treatment agenda indicated his level of commitment and motivation in treatment. As long as his depression was in check, Dan was a highly motivated and engaged client.

As we neared the end of his first year in therapy, Dan once again struggled with his moods. He could not understand how he could attend therapy regularly and be motivated to change, yet still feel depressed. At times, he continued to be overwhelmed by low self-esteem, shame, and hopelessness. At other times, he was bright, cheerful, and hopeful. Dan rode the proverbial emotional roller coaster, sometimes from week to week. He was working hard in therapy, practicing his self-help strategies, but consistent change did not occur. Obviously, Dan's depression hindered meaningful change.

Dan kept pushing on in therapy. He enjoyed focusing his energy on what it would be like if he could relate to himself and his wife as a secure, well-adjusted adult. We spent time working on these issues and he developed more confidence, less self-consciousness, and a sense of freedom from his childhood issues and patterns. When Dan was symptom-free, he and Ellen got along nicely. They would occasionally utilize couple's dialogue, but often found it unnecessary. Ellen expressed hope that his positive mood was permanent. However, his progress was typically short-lived. Every six or seven sessions, Dan would crash into a depressive state that would last for weeks or months. There seemed to be no end in sight.

After a two-month break in therapy, Dan and Ellen returned for a follow-up session and reported that he had been symptom-free for four months and they were communicating better than ever. Their therapy (individual and couple) had been a long grind, nearly eighteen months. Finally, they experienced consistent success. At that point, we agreed to discontinue therapy. They were thrilled.

I advised Dan to maintain contact with his doctor, continue taking his medication, and work on their communication. Dan wanted to know when he could stop taking medication. I suggested that once his symptoms appeared to stay in complete remission, he should talk with his doctor about the possibility of discontinuing his medication. I encouraged them to work closely with their doctors, to ask questions, and communicate openly. We left therapy agreeing that they could call me anytime if they needed to talk, or schedule a "refresher" session. I hoped that I would not see them again. I was wrong.

Questions

Dan and Ellen had the financial resources and/or excellent insurance coverage that allowed them to participate in long-term treatment, individually and as a couple. However, most practitioners do not work in private practice settings where this is possible. Many practitioners, especially those just out of school, work in publicly funded programs that serve clients without financial resources, or in other settings where managed care limitations disallow the length of treatment described so far in this case.

1. How would treatment differ if they did not have the resources to engage in long-term treatment? With what approaches or models would you treat Dan and Ellen if their circumstances were different? Use the practice literature and classroom discussion to address this dilemma.

Dan did not seem to be responding to his medication. While he had periods of remission, he moved back and forth between symptom relief and apparent depression. Given these facts, as described by the author,

2. Using the professional literature and your experience, make a list of the possible reasons for Dan's problems in treatment. Based on this list, what likely reasons exist for his problems?

3. Based on the discussion above, what course of action would you take to address his progress, or lack thereof? Be specific, and defend your position and plan.

Relapse and New Diagnosis

After seven months of continued symptom relief, Dan plummeted into a depression that left him bedridden for three days. His anger at Ellen returned and he became overwhelmed with shame and guilt at his behavior. Dan and Ellen returned to therapy, seeking support and encouragement.

He reported that his medication no longer worked. We agreed that Dan might benefit from seeing a psychiatrist. I referred him to my consulting psychiatrist and sent an introductory letter explaining Dan's recurring symptoms, medications already tried, and outcomes. Dr. Farr assumed the role of changing and adjusting medications in an attempt to treat Dan's worsening depressive symptoms.

To my surprise, Dr Farr rediagnosed Dan with Bipolar II Disorder and placed him on a form of lithium, along with an antidepressant medication. Of the two to three million people in the United States diagnosed with a Bipolar Disorder, approximately 60 percent have Bipolar II versus Bipolar I Disorder. Bipolar I Disorder includes one or more episodes of major depression and at least one manic or mixed episode (Quinn, 2000).

Bipolar II Disorder is a subtler form of Bipolar I and includes one or more episodes of major depression alternating with at least one hypo-manic episode. Hypo-mania is less debilitating than mania. The highs are not as grandiose or persistently elevated. Practitioners often misdiagnose Bipolar I because clients do not recognize their hypo-manic behaviors as problematic. They feel energized, productive, and creative. In fact, they are often reluctant to treat their disorder because of the benefits they experience during these episodes.

For example, I once had a 31-year-old, married, female client in treatment for biochemical depression without consistent benefit. She was despondent and overwhelmed by her new baby. During one session, she began telling a story about a period shortly after the birth of her baby.

I had a somewhat difficult pregnancy, probably because it was my first. I stayed in the hospital for two days, feeling pretty wiped out. Once I got home though I felt myself become so excited about having a new baby that I became very energetic and creative. I spent the next couple of days putting up all kinds of Christmas decorations and lights, inside and out.

Then I got a great idea that I wanted to paint a mural on the baby's bedroom wall but I realized the fumes could be harmful, so I decided to paint it on the wall next to the steps leading to the downstairs rec room. This made sense because we had decided that this would be the baby's play area.

For the next three days, that's what I did. I painted a 15-foot mural. I would work on it non-stop, except to tend to the baby. When my husband came home, I'd have him do baby care so that I could paint more. One night I stayed up until 4 a.m. Everyone who came over said that they couldn't believe what I had done, especially with a new baby. I'm not that artistic so this was amazing to me too.

Revised Treatment

Once Dr. Farr made the Bipolar II diagnosis, we identified Dan's heretofore unseen hypo-manic episodes. The DSM-IV-TR, defines Bipolar II as hypo-mania associated with one or more major depressive episodes. Hypo-mania must include at least three of the following symptoms:

1. Inflated self-esteem or grandiosity
2. Decreased need for sleep
3. More talkative than usual
4. Flight of ideas or subjective experience that thoughts are racing
5. Distractibility
6. Increased activity
7. Excessive involvement in pleasurable activities with a high potential for painful consequences.

For example, several times a year Dan would become overinvolved in a work project. He would stay at work throughout the night diligently trying to accomplish his goals. His mood would elevate and he felt energized and positive. He once received a special acknowledgment for his hard work. Ellen said that Dan appeared more able to communicate during these times. After engaging in this behavior for several weeks or months, he would end up fighting angrily with Ellen over his inability to tend to home chores because he was "burned out." Small disagreements would grow into major altercations with Dan inappropriately acting out. This would lead to a return of overwhelming depression. For the weeks following his new diagnosis and medication regimen, Dan seemed to progress symptom-free. Perhaps we had finally found the correct combination of medication and therapy.

Ellen's Individual Therapy

During this period, Ellen decided to attend individual sessions to vent her frustrations and work on locating and using a new social support network outside the marriage. While I encouraged her to feel hopeful about Dan's recovery, she was tired. In fact, she and I shared frustration about the seriousness of his disorder and its resistance to treatment. During our session, I realized that I was struggling with the need to accept the limits of my ability to help. I had become emotionally involved with Dan and Ellen and felt frustrated by my inability to do more for them.

Ellen found it more difficult to persevere. Despite the meaningful work in individual therapy, Dan continued to cycle through bouts with mild, moderate, and severe depression related to his marital problems, his biochemistry, his unwillingness to reach out for help, and his newly discovered tendency to stop taking his medication. The severe episodes of depression continued to take their toll on their marriage. Ellen feared that the marriage would end. Finally, she asked for a marital separation as an ultimatum, demanding that he make major changes.

I recommended that Ellen purchase a self-help book, *How You Can Survive When They're Depressed* (Sheffield, 1998). I use this book with spouses coping with depression. Ellen was further concerned about how their arguing and Dan's problems affected their daughter.

She was burning out. Her love and sympathy were not enough to cure the disorder and she grew more despondent as she sank into her grief. I also encouraged Ellen to contact friends and begin meeting for coffee or dinner away from Dan, even hiring a babysitter or allowing her parents to watch their daughter if she had to. It is important for spouses in these circumstances to have social outlets outside the home. It helps bring balance, perspective, and support during extremely difficult times.

Major Crisis

One day I received a crisis call from Ellen. Dan had gone to bed three days prior, and had not gotten up except to briefly eat and go to the bathroom. He had not showered or taken his medicine. He had missed work and did not appear to be improving. She stated that she had tried to engage him in a dialogue about what he wanted and needed but he responded with anger and tears. I referred them for psychiatric hospitalization. Dan sounded more serious than ever.

I contacted Dr. Farr to check my assessment and alert him to the whereabouts of his patient. He admitted Dan to the hospital for five days. While inpatient he received positive therapeutic support. He attended educational classes on the management of depression, medication compliance, and stress management. He met with a caseworker who coordinated with the psychiatrist regarding his medication. Ellen and Dan also met with a therapist who helped them find solutions for avoiding future hospitalizations. Following discharge, Dan returned home to Ellen and their child in a positive, nondepressed state of mind. Once again, Ellen and Dan were hopeful about their marriage. She stopped considering a separation.

Over the next few months, we cycled through the same issues we worked on earlier. I often reiterated techniques and themes that Dan, Ellen, and I had explored numerous times. At times, Dan appeared motivated for change, at other times he did not. I tried to influence his motivation by encouraging him to schedule follow-up appointments, calling him to reschedule when he failed to appear, speaking to him after receiving a crisis call from his wife, and verbally contracting with him to attend regular sessions. His wife took on the responsibility of reaching out for intervention when Dan could not.

Over time, it became clear that Dan routinely ignored early warning signals that indicated an onset of severe symptoms. His inability or unwillingness to recognize pending danger and to take appropriate steps became problematic. This became a central focus of therapy. After a crisis, Ellen and Dan would attend a conjoint session and Dan would sheepishly explain how he had not paid close enough attention to his emerging symptoms. He had been working too many hours, not had enough sleep, and/or had not refilled his prescription. Ellen began believing that she was working harder than Dan was to fix his disorder.

Crisis Leads to Breakthrough

A couple of weeks later, Ellen again called in crisis. Dan was experiencing his worst depressive episode. He arose only to go to the bathroom, would not eat, missed work, and grumbled at Ellen when she tried to speak with him about his plans for pulling himself out of the depression. Ellen was willing to do whatever he needed, but was unclear about what to do with him. She had already spoken with Dan about returning to the psychiatric hospital. He responded by pulling the bedcovers over his head and yelling at her to leave him alone. Later that day he got out of bed, dressed, and told Ellen that he was leaving and she would never see him again. He got in the car and sat there sobbing in the driveway. Since Dan was not functioning and Ellen had to work that evening, she called his parents to watch their daughter. When they arrived, she went to the car and they talked. Dan agreed to call his psychiatrist.

Just prior to this crisis, Dan had not attended a therapy session for over three months. He had stopped taking his mood stabilizer because it made him feel "fuzzy-headed," and had not consulted his psychiatrist while making this decision. The return of his severe depressive symptoms several weeks after discontinuing medication was predictable because of his history.

During the follow-up session after the latest crisis, Ellen mentioned that Dan had also neglected to refill his other prescriptions and had gone without them for four days. I confronted Dan's behavior and insisted that he comply with his medication regime. The next day Dan contacted his doctor. The psychiatrist represcribed his mood stabilizer and other medications. Within five days, Dan's symptoms subsided and he was functioning appropriately. Dan lapsed into a significant medical crisis because of his "normal" depression combined with withdrawal symptoms caused by his discontinuing medication abruptly.

At this point in treatment, Dan finally decided to incorporate all of the techniques he had gained in therapy. He maintained benefit from the therapeutic dose of medication he was now taking daily. Although the mood stabilizer caused some ongoing side effects, he dealt with them in a more appropriate manner after realizing how necessary this medicine was for controlling his symptoms. Dan said that he was finally tired of feeling sick and tired, and was willing to do whatever it took to help himself feel better and preserve his family. For some reason, this latest crisis made Dan realize that he was worth saving.

Now that Dan was taking responsibility for managing his illness, he decided to explore his resistance to asking for help. He had learned to rely only on himself as a child, trusting no one. His pride prevented him from admitting his struggles. He kept hoping that he could manage his symptoms on his own, so that nobody would think less of him. Dan was now aware that this error in judgment led to his ignoring his early warning signs of depression. He was now ready to reach out to others as needed.

When Dan managed his depressive symptoms, his family life responded accordingly. He and Ellen enjoyed their time together and Ellen felt hopeful about their future. Ellen had little reason to feel angry and resentful, which softened her tone making her less likely to trigger Dan's defenses. Dan could balance his family's needs with his own and rarely neglected Ellen or his daughters.

Unlike Major Depression, a bipolar diagnosis is often chronic with mild expectation of full remission. Management of symptoms, rather than introspection is usually the primary focus of treatment. Unlike Bipolar I Disorder, a Bipolar II diagnosis is more difficult for clients to accept because of the moderate nature of the manic episodes, and resistance is common. Usually, active self-management does not occur until a major crisis occurs. This is exactly what happened to Dan.

Reflections on Dan and Ellen

At this point, Dan and Ellen had been in treatment on and off for four years. Since his employer was self-insured, they had generous mental health benefits, which allowed us to do long-term psychotherapy. For the last two years, my primary role was case manager and crisis interventionist. I originally speculated that they needed a ten to fifteen week course of therapy. I had not foreseen that they would continue this long. I also miscalculated the seriousness of Dan's intractable mental disorder.

I wondered if my own lack of boundaries opened the door for the recurring need for crisis intervention. Therapists who set clear boundaries are less likely to struggle with clients who abuse the process by reaching out for ego-supportive intervention and advice when they are in a crisis. This was an issue in my therapy with Dan. However, it was usually Ellen and not Dan who contacted me seeking guidance. I encouraged Dan to feel safe enough to contact me at the earliest signs of trouble yet he had not accomplished this goal once in our therapy.

I was supportive and respectful and tolerant of his disabling distress and dysfunction, perhaps too tolerant. I wanted to establish a contract with significant consequences if he ignored early warning signs or did not reach out in advance of a crisis. However, what could be more severe than his depressive crises and possible divorce? I decided that I did not have the power to enforce consequences, except possibly terminating treatment. I did not want to confront that ethical issue.

Questions

The author just described her issues with the treatment. She wondered if she had become too close or too involved with the clients, perhaps to their detri-

ment. Given the fact that this issue commonly occurs in practice, let's look at the issue before proceeding.

1. Explore the professional code of ethics (NASW, 2000) and best practice literature searching for the profession's position on boundaries, limit-setting, and the consequences of terminating clients early for noncompliance. Be sure to look at this issue from as many different sides as possible.

2. Based on this exploration, what is your position on the author's discussion above? What are the various issues involved in determining your course of action? What will you do when you are faced with a similar circumstance (because you will be faced with this; we all are)?

3. Critique the author's work. What strengths and problems can you identify in how the author handled this issue pertaining to Dan and Ellen? Defend your positions.

For nearly 20 years, I have provided managed care services with an emphasis on short-term therapy. Short-term therapy models focus on the here-and-now, with delineated, measurable goals and outcomes. The therapist is authoritative but not authoritarian. The client-therapist relationship is demystified as the relationship takes on a psycho-educational tone (Austad, 1994).

My style is usually flexible and eclectic, as demonstrated by the variety of approaches I used with Dan and Ellen. I encourage autonomy and independence, rather than transference and dependence. I always expected that they reach their goals efficiently. It simply did not happen with any consistency, primarily because of Dan's disorder and his frequent refusal to take medication daily. Dan's case was especially frustrating for me. Usually when a client is clinically depressed, it is plausible to assume that relief comes from medication and/or therapy. There is easy-to-treat depression and difficult-to-treat depression. Dan had the second, and he often did not medicate properly. These factors made this a frustrating and difficult case, indeed.

What initially appeared as simple-to-treat marital discord evolved into difficult-to-treat bipolar II disorder. Dan came close to losing his marriage, his job, and his life before he was willing to invest in meaningful efforts to manage his disorder. One has to wonder what is next for this couple. They certainly have predictable patterns; however, the change in Dan's attitude and behavior could be the turning point that dramatically influences the course of his disorder, and his life.

Questions

The author presented an interesting, successfully terminated case that involved many issues commonly found in mental health practice. Taking a broad view of this case, reevaluate the author's work and your participation through the questions asked throughout the case.

1. **Take a moment to review Dan and Ellen's progress in treatment. Based on the author's description, the professional literature, and the latest practice evidence, what occurred to account for her clients' progress.**

2. **What was the theoretical approach or combination of approaches that appeared to work best for Dan and Ellen?**

3. **Based on the work you have done earlier, what additional intervention(s) would you recommend? Use the literature and latest evidence to justify your recommendations.**

4. **Overall, what is your professional opinion of the work performed in this case? As always, refer to the professional literature, practice evidence, your experience, and the experience of student-colleagues when developing your opinion.**

5. **Based on this review, what additional or alternative approaches could have been used with this case? That is, if you were the practitioner, how would you have approached this case? Please explain and justify your approach.**

6. **What did this case demonstrate that you could use in other practice settings. List the most important things you learned and how they might help in your practice career.**

Bibliography

American Psychiatric Association (2000). *Diagnostic and statistical manual of mental disorders* (4th ed., TR). Washington, DC: Author.

Austad, C. S. (1994). *Is long-term psychotherapy unethical?* San Francisco: Jossey-Bass.

Beck, J. S. (1995). *Cognitive therapy: Basics and beyond.* New York: Girlfriend Press.

DePaulo, R. J. (2002). *Understanding depression.* New York: Wiley.

Evans, K., & Sullivan, J. M. (2001). *Dual diagnosis: Counseling the mentally ill substance abuser* (2nd ed.). New York: Guilford.

Ginsberg, L., Nackerud, L., & Larrison, C. R. (2004). *Human biology for social workers: Development, genetics, and health.* Boston: Allyn and Bacon.

Johnson, J. L. (2004). *Fundamentals of substance abuse practice.* Pacific Grove, CA: Brooks/Cole.

Kaufman, G. (1992). *Shame: The power of caring.* Rochester, VT: Schankman Books.

Luguet, W. (1996). *Short-term couples therapy.* New York: Brunner/Mazel.

National Association of Social Workers (2000). *Code of Ethics of the National Association of Social Workers.* Washington, DC: Author.

Quinn, B. P. (2000). *The depression sourcebook.* Lincolnwood, Il: Lowell House.

Sheffield, A. (1998). *How you can survive when they're depressed.* New York: Three Rivers Press.

Tolman, A. O. (2001). *Depression in adults.* Kansas City, MO: Compact Clinical.

Turner, F. J. (1996). *Social work treatment* (4th ed.). New York: The Free Press.

Carletta

Patricia Stowe Bolea

I met Carletta and her family while practicing as an outpatient social worker in my home state of Indiana. Carletta's case demonstrates the importance of assuming an advanced generalist approach to problem behavior in adolescents. Basing my assessment and treatment decisions on information obtained about Carletta's multi-systemic environment, I linked Carletta's chronic diabetes to adolescent development, psychological development, as well as the family, their religious beliefs, and the larger culture, including issues unique to the region where they lived and worked. Had we not integrated information from these various sources into her assessment, Carletta may not have improved.

Presenting Problems

Carletta's school counselor referred her to therapy for an unusual problem. A teacher caught her sticking other students with straight pins in the hallway of her school. While this had occurred several times, school personnel only caught her once. The school counselor thought Carletta could benefit from counseling.

Carletta arrived with her family for our first session. She was a polite and happy 16-year-old adolescent young woman. Carletta was well-groomed, wearing jeans and a colorful sweater. She was slightly overweight, with a clear complexion and a bright smile. She made good eye contact while we talked and was not shy, as many adolescents are when meeting a therapist for the first time. She quickly and freely engaged in our conversation. I noticed that her social skills seemed advanced for a young woman her age.

Carletta forthrightly acknowledged the pin-sticking incidents at school, but also denied any additional problems. Carletta reported that everything was fine at school, home, and with her friends at school. She stated that she had "no idea" why she was meeting with me, since she had no problems in her life.

Prior to our first meeting, I spoke privately with her parents to collect background information. Mr. and Mrs. Brown expressed concern about Carletta's recent pin-sticking behavior in school. According to her parents, a teacher caught Carletta sticking other students with straight pins in the crowded hallway between classes at school. Apparently, several students had complained about being stuck with pins. However, both students and school personnel were unsure who did it. One student suspected Carletta, but could not prove it. Later that week, a teacher on hallway duty observed Carletta sticking another student as she passed by her locker. Carletta's school counselor spoke with both Carletta and her parents about the incident, and referred them to me for treatment.

Questions

Given the unusual nature of this presenting problem, answer the following questions before moving ahead with this case.

1. What is your first hunch regarding the presenting problem? Explore the practice literature and discuss this issue with other students to find the prevalence of this type of behavior. If the literature does not speak specifically about this problem, are there other problems or categories of problems that this behavior fits with pertaining to treatment?

2. What is the next direction of inquiry and assessment? Further, explore the practice literature to locate theories or models that apply to this type of behavior in adolescent girls. Based on the approaches you find, what information would you need to collect to perform a comprehensive and/or multi-systemic assessment? (See Chapter 1).

3. What personal strengths can you locate and name at this early juncture in treatment?

During my first session with Carletta, I focused primarily on engagement (Murphy & Dillon, 2003). This came easily for both of us. As previously mentioned, she was bright and skilled in speaking with adults. She willingly answered questions and was comfortable engaging in a conversation about her life and problems. Rather than conducting a formal assessment, I approached our initial session as an opportunity to build rapport by getting to know her. After engaging her, I could proceed to gathering the information I needed to complete my assessment and construct an appropriate treatment plan.

I encouraged Carletta to tell me about herself, including the things she wished others knew about her. I asked questions about her family and personal history. I also asked about school. Carletta spoke comfortably about her family, claiming that she loved her family, and that most of the time they got along "very" well. She noted that sometimes they argued. Carletta believed that her parents were "too strict." However, she did not express hostility toward her parents, something I am used to seeing from adolescents in therapy. Instead, she said that she didn't feel any differently about her parents than most of her friends felt about theirs. She further said that she understood that the strict rules were her parent's way of letting her know that they loved her and wanted her safe. Carletta made these comments sincerely. What teenager does that?

Carletta also got along well with her 11-year-old brother. She had a "couple" of good friends at school, who also attended the church where her father ministered. She enjoyed her friends, and claimed to "really" like going to church. The Brown family was heavily involved in the church. Mr. Brown was a pastor at a local Christian church. Over the years, the family had lived in three different towns in Indiana, where Mr. Brown pastored to his congregations. He pastored in two churches in southern Indiana for six years each. He had been at their current church in suburban Indianapolis for three years.

Carletta spoke openly and happily about being a Christian. She enjoyed her church friends and church-related activities. She said that her father was a well-respected pastor whose congregation looked up to him. She expressed pride at her father's work and the family's commitment to God.

When I asked how she liked high school, Carletta stopped smiling. She said that sometimes school was difficult, mainly because of the cliques in her school. However, her smile returned when she spoke about how her "church friends" at school made it easier for her to fit in. She said that the popular girls referred to her and her friends as "goody-two-shoes." Carletta said that she didn't mind this, because she was proud of mostly "doing the right things." While she did not mention sticking others with pins as part of "doing right," she did say that she did not want to gain a "reputation" for drinking or having sex like many of the other kids. She said she did not care what others thought of her because she openly expressed her faith.

Apparently, Carletta was an excellent student. She enjoyed her school work, and found that much of it came easy to her. Her parents had encouraged her to study hard. The only problem she had with school was that her teachers gave too much homework. Finally, Carletta sounded like a normal teenager! She was unsure of whether her plans included college or more involvement in her father's church. She claimed that she had time to figure all of that out later.

During this initial session, I remained in the position of empathic listener, using reflection and gentle probing skills to keep her talking about her life and enhance our initial engagement (Murphy & Dillon, 2003). As we approached the end of our first session, I asked about her sticking people with pins. Carletta laughed, and said that she knew it was a "silly" thing to do. She said that she was very sorry for doing it, and didn't mean for it to be such a "big deal." When I asked why she did it, Carletta said she didn't know for sure. She repeated that she was sorry, and referred to it as a "silly prank."

At this point, Carletta began exhibiting different affect. While she spoke about her sorrow, Carletta appeared frustrated and embarrassed by all the attention she received because of this incident. She also allowed a hint of anger to show, yet she ended the conversation as it began, smiling.

Psychosocial History

When I met with Mr. and Mrs. Brown, they offered a detailed history of Carletta's growth and development. Mr. Brown presented as a 43-year-old, tall and slender man, normally dressed in business attire, always with shirt and tie. Mrs. Brown was an attractive woman in her early forties with a sweet disposition. She was slightly overweight and often dressed in pantsuits or casual dresses. They looked the part of the local pastor and wife.

It was obvious to me that Carletta's family provided love, care, and attention over the years. They had kept careful records from school and her doctors. They said that everyone who knew her called Carletta an ideal daughter, student, sibling, and friend. As stated earlier, she earned excellent grades in school and was active in extracurricular activities such as scouting, band, and church. Her parents could not understand why Carletta did something so unusual in school. According to her parents, acting out was definitely out of character for Carletta.

The Browns also spoke at length about their family's deep commitment to their Christian faith, as one would expect from a pastor and his wife. They spoke about God's blessings in their lives, including the many moves over the years from one church to another, as God called Mr. Brown to serve. While they said that the moves caused temporary disruption for the kids, God always provided and helped make transitions from one community to another smooth and enjoyable.

Juvenile Diabetes

At age six, Carletta was diagnosed with Juvenile Diabetes. Mr. and Mrs. Brown were especially proud of the way Carletta managed her diabetic condition. Both parents discussed the difficulty everyone, especially Carletta, had adjusting to her condition in the early years. Before Indianapolis, they lived in small towns and worked with small congregations. This enabled Mr. and Mrs. Brown to remain physically close to Carletta in case a medical emergency occurred in school or during church activities. Being close helped the family manage their worry over her rigorous dietary requirements and daily, multiple insulin injections. Mr. and Mrs. Brown prided themselves in the way Carletta treated her illness. Because she was a responsible young woman, Carletta always remained compliant with her diet and insulin injections. They also praised God for watching over Carletta and keeping her healthy and happy despite her chronic disease.

Questions

Now that the author has presented more information about Carletta and her family, and before reading the author's assessment, perform the following exercises based on your education, experience, the professional literature, and the available best practice evidence. To increase your learning potential, you may want to do this in a small group with other students in your course.

1. Based on the information contained above, construct a three-generation genogram and eco-map that represents Carletta's personal, familial, and environmental circumstances. What further information do you need to complete this exercise? What patterns do these two important graphical assessment tools demonstrate?

2. Building on your earlier work; complete a list of Carletta's issues and strengths, drawing from multi-systemic sources.

3. Write a two- to three-page narrative assessment that encompasses Carletta's multi-systemic issues and strengths. Review Chapter 1 if needed. This narrative should provide a comprehensive and multi-systemic explanation of their life as they prepare to undergo therapy with the author. Below we offer a few questions to guide this process:
   - What are your hunches regarding Carletta's view of her self as a daughter and developing young woman?
   - What are your hunches about her feelings regarding her adolescent identity and her diabetes?
   - What are your hunches regarding her ability to be honest in her relationship with her parents?
   - What are your hunches about the role their religious faith and Mr. Brown's professional role plays in Carletta's issues and strengths?

4. Try to identify the theoretical model or approach that you use to guide your assessment. According to the literature, what other theoretical options are available and how would these change the nature of your assessment?

5. End by developing multi-axial DSM-IV-TR diagnoses for both Carletta. Provide a list of client symptoms that you used to justify your diagnostic decision. What, if any, information was missing that would make this easier?

Multi-Systemic Assessment

Advanced Generalist Perspective

I use an Advanced Generalist perspective to organize my thinking and actions in clinical practice. Similar to the Advanced Multi-Systemic approach described in

Chapter 1, advanced generalist practitioners focus client assessment on person-in-environment, meaning we examine how people interact, influence, and are influenced by their environment. Client assessment considers how factors from multiple systems interact to comprise a holistic definition of client problems and strengths. At the individual and family level, the goal is to understand the client's perspective.

With Carletta, my goal was to understand her as a developing adolescent managing a chronic disease, who happened to stick classmates with a straight pin. In other words, how did she experience her life and what factors contributed to her acting in a way that everyone said was out of her character? Moreover, how did her parents experience their role as parents and caregivers, and what factors contributed to how they handled this particular issue and family issues in general?

For Carletta, a 16-year-old high school student with diabetes, all reports indicated that she had managed her disease well. By all accounts, and in my opinion, Carletta was a "good kid" who somehow decided to act in a way that landed her in trouble at school. At first glance, she was a happy, relatively well-adjusted teenager with a strong religious faith and loving, caring parents. Given the glowing reports, the question remained about why she acted out at this time in her life. I was also interested to understand the potential meaning behind her acting out. In other words, what did Carletta's specific behavior mean in the context of her life?

Questions

In his work pertaining to families and family therapy, Jay Haley (1976; 1980) stated that a family's presenting symptoms, particularly when children were the perpetrators, usually represented a metaphor for other, sometimes more significant issues in the family. He claimed that understanding the metaphoric meaning of a family's presenting problems provided practitioners with valuable clues about overall family functioning and can provide clues about possible intervention planning with families. In the exercise below, use this approach to look at Carletta in the context of her family.

1. Locate and read Haley's ideas pertaining to the meaning of symptoms in family assessment and treatment.

2. Develop a list of possible metaphors that define Carletta's presenting problem related to herself, adolescent development, and/or her family system.

As parents, Mr. and Mrs. Brown appeared to manage her growth and independence by being part of and close to extrafamilial systems that Carletta participated in on a daily basis. This allowed her parents to play a consistent and central role in her growth, development, and outside participation. At this point, I could not tell whether they were overprotective, since that is a matter of individual definition and not an objective concept. However, they were not underinvolved in her life. Yet, it would be misleading to compare their situation to other families with 16-year-old daughters. Because of her diabetes and the daily regimen its care required, high levels of parental involvement are typically needed and often medically necessary to facilitate the healthy maintenance of a diabetic child in school and/or extracurricular activities.

Their role in Carletta's life was relatively easy when she was younger and they lived in small communities. However, high school presented the family a different and difficult challenge. Carletta naturally experienced more peer-related pressure to fit in and belong (Kelly & Hansen, 1987). Moreover, because of her "normal" need for increasing independence, her parents were unable to protect and/or oversee her life in the same ways as before.

Medical Issues.   Advanced generalist practitioners educate themselves about any medical condition a client experiences, particularly chronic conditions. According to the Juvenile Diabetes Research Foundation, more than one million Americans have juvenile (type 1) diabetes. This disease occurs with sudden onset and makes its victims insulin-dependent for life. Type 1 diabetes also carries the constant threat of devastating complications, even if the person maintains the proper diet and medication. In type 1 diabetes, a person's pancreas produces little or no insulin. Some researchers believe that the human body's immune system actually attacks and destroys insulin-producing cells in the pancreas. Type 1 diabetes is not caused by obesity or eating excessive sugar, two common myths that many people believe (http://www.jdrf.org/index.cfm).

One never outgrows this disease. Insulin permits people to live, however it does not cure their diabetes. As a lifelong, chronic, and progressive disease, the best people can do is holding it in remission with proper daily care. Some of the eventual and devastating effects may include kidney failure, blindness, nerve damage, amputations, heart attack, and stroke (http://www.jdrf.org/index.cfm).

The daily management routine Carletta and her family managed included multiple insulin injections as well as blood sugar tests conducted by pricking her fingers six or more times per day. While trying to balance insulin injections with her food intake, Carletta and her family needed to be prepared for potential hypoglycemic (low blood sugar) and hyperglycemic (high blood sugar) reactions, which could be deadly. Additionally, many other factors can negatively affect a person's blood-sugar control including stress, hormonal changes, periods of growth, physical activity, medications, illness/infection, and fatigue (Jack, 2003). For the practitioner, this information is important, however, what is more salient is the psychological or emotional response of the people who are affected. In my case, that meant Carletta and her family members.

One way to understand the impact of diabetes is to examine testimonial data. According to the chairman of the JDRF,

> I've had juvenile diabetes for over 30 years. It changes everything about a person's life. And to add to the day-in, day-out hassles of living with diabetes—the balancing of diet, exercise, and insulin, the shots, the terrible episodes of low blood sugar, the weird

feelings of high blood sugar—is the knowledge that even if you do all you can to be as normal as possible, you're not, you're different, and you face the uncertainty of a life visited upon by early death, blindness, kidney failure, amputation, heart attack or stroke.

A 26-year-old in New Yorker wrote, "Diabetes is always there. There's never a vacation. It's a like a bad dream that lasts all day, all year, for my entire life." From a 13-year-old in California,

> I am thirteen years old and I can't imagine having diabetes for the rest of my life. I can't imagine going blind and never seeing my parents' faces or flowers or my animals. I can't imagine losing a leg and never being able to dance or walk normally again. I can't imagine giving myself shots for the rest of my life. (http://www.jdrf.org/index. cfm)

Given this information, I needed to ask many more questions about how Carletta and her family handled their situation. For example, I did not see any indication of the stress and/or frustration the literature discussed. Where was Carletta's anger and frustration related to her chronic disease? What about her parents' anger or exhaustion; they did not complain during our session either. I believed that it was important to note any period of acting out or emotional expressions of sadness, fear, or anger by Carletta or her family, since their initial presentation was happiness. Perhaps these feelings did not exist. What's written in the professional literature certainly does not apply to everyone. Maybe this family was an exception. I made this the focus of our next session.

Tentative Ideas

Carletta and her family presented a happy story about a child with chronic illness, who happened to act out in school in an unusual manner. In fact, the family presented Carletta as a raving success story that seemed better suited for public testimonial than for a girl accused of assaulting other students with stickpins. This might be the case. This family might have utilized their strengths of love, cohesiveness, and faith at home, and social support in church, school, and community to manage their problems (Saleebey, 1997) and accomplish this feat.

My other hunch was that Carletta experienced hidden, yet smoldering anger regarding her illness and all it entailed. Rather than directly confronting or discussing this with her family, friends, school personnel, or me, Carletta kept it bottled up inside, ultimately, leading her to "stick" other kids with pins as a way of expressing what the literature and I considered normal emotional reactions to her medical condition. That is, I surmised that the pins she used were a metaphor about her anger at having to "stick" herself with needles everyday. In the absence of other ways to express her anger, Carletta forced others to feel the needle as she did everyday of her life. To investigate this hunch, I felt it appropriate to examine her family's interactions in the context of life stage and/or family development (Carter & McGoldrick, 1988). In other words, why did Carletta have trouble expressing normal emotions in her family?

Family and Culture

It was important to understand Carletta and her family within the context of their geography, race, culture, and religious background. I knew that her family was comprised of a Caucasian, heterosexual couple with two children living in Indiana. What I did not know was the impact of their culture and environment. This area of investigation is important to anyone approaching clients from an advanced generalist perspective.

To understand the Browns, it was important to understand them in the context of geography, as well as regional and local culture. I needed to consider traditions of the midwest and the south. While the state of Indiana lays north of the Ohio River (technically north of the Mason-Dixon Line) many of the prevailing cultural beliefs and practices, particularly south of Indianapolis, is dominated by southern sensibilities and beliefs. In other words, while Indiana's location makes it part of the Corn Belt, the Bible Belt influences its culture.

For my work with Carletta and her family, this meant that I needed to explore the values of Bible Belt Christians related to their dominant and unquestioned expectation of traditional family structure and religious practices, coupled with traditional gender roles. Without an understanding of how these values worked in their family, I would not be able to work with the Browns.

Gender Roles

As stated earlier, Carletta's father was a Christian minister, often expected to be the local beacon for conservative family values, including patriarchal family relationship structures. As I spoke with the family, I began developing the belief that Mr. Brown possessed and exercised unquestioned power in family decision making, leaving Mrs. Brown with dominion over household decisions. As a pastor's wife, she worked full-time (as a host or organizer) for the church without salary. Part of traditional gender socialization required hard work without questioning authority, and being happy about the arrangement. In other words, Mrs. Brown, and soon Carletta, could not be anything but happy about serving their husband and father, as well as the church and Father. Their autonomy and creativity were expressed through domesticity (Hunter College Women's Studies Collective, 1995; Lipman-Blumen, 1984).

Within this context, it was important to explore whether members of the Brown family expressed anger or any "negative" emotion. Typically, in such traditional families, females are socialized to be "nice" above all, conditioned to stifle any emotions that run contrary to the socially accepted polite or demure "lady" (Lipman-Blumen, 1984). I decided to approach the family with the assumption that while Carletta and her family had managed her illness by dutifully following prescribed treatment regimens of diet, medicines, injections, and follow-up appointments with physicians, their emotional needs required attention in the context of their family structure and religious background.

Further, as Carletta approached adolescence, her growing need for independence and acceptance at school was juxtaposed against her need for family care and support for her illness. Additionally, the expectation that she always be "ladylike" collided with her normal feelings of anger about her illness, and desire to be "like" other students.

Their religious beliefs added yet another layer to our work. Members of the Brown family maintained a strong, personal relationship with God. They believed that when people experience emotional or psychological pain, they had "spiritual problems" needing prayer. Hence, psychology, counseling, or mental health was not necessarily trusted or considered helpful with such matters.

Therefore, when Carletta experienced anger or sadness, or even the isolation caused by her illness, she learned to define it as something "bad" in her that she must make right with God. There was no vehicle to help her understand these feelings as normal or expected. Nobody had ever given Carletta permission to be angry. She learned to mute her anger and not acknowledge its presence in her life. Subsequently, Carletta acted out her anger, as most adolescents do because they do not have the language, skills, or freedom to express themselves (Siepker & Kandaras, 1985). Thus, as Carletta gave herself numerous shots each day, she acted out her anger by sticking other kids with pins instead of talking about it.

I also had to consider my ability to engage the Browns in therapy, since their religious beliefs discouraged anything except prayer. I needed to monitor our relationship closely to ensure that they were actually working, and not simply attending to save public "face" or to please the school.

Questions

Compare the assessment and diagnostic statement you developed earlier to the author's. Where do you find points of agreement and disagreement? Discuss these issues with student-colleagues and use the professional literature to analyze the differences.

1. **What implications for treatment arise because of the differences between your assessment and diagnoses and the author's?**

2. **Explain these differences as part of a treatment plan. That is, develop a treatment plan for Carletta based on your assessment. Include the types of treatment needed, theoretical model(s), or approach(es) you would use, and how these differ from those used by the author.**

Treatment Issues

Based on my assessment described earlier, it was time to proceed with treatment. I worked with Carletta for approximately three months, from intake to termination. She attended six individual sessions during that period. In addition to the intake session, we also conducted four family therapy sessions.

As Carletta and I began treatment, I worked on engagement and relationship development, gently exploring her life experience with diabetes. At first, she fluctuated between reticence and minimizing her experiences. Finally, she began voicing the unpleasantness of her daily routine. Once she began expressing her feelings, our relationship grew, allowing me to lead a direct discussion about her increasing discomfort. Since she became a teenager, Carletta grew embarrassed by her parent's concern and constant supervision of her injection regimen. She was fully aware of the conflict between needing her parents' help and wanting independence. Carletta wanted more independence and freedom from her parents, while simultaneously recognizing how helpful and supportive they had always been for her.

Likewise, Carletta began talking about her desire to be normal and without disease. She told stories about other kids teasing her, and being embarrassed by the way teachers assisted with her diet and medication. She talked about how she tried to hide her disease from friends at high school. I found the change in our relationship interesting. Once I provided her freedom to speak openly about herself, Carletta had no problem expressing her sadness, embarrassment, and frustration. However, when asked about any feelings of anger, she would shut down, smile, and minimize.

Early family sessions proved equally successful with everything except anger. Both Mr. and Mrs. Brown openly discussed their fear, sadness, and isolation. Both parents said that they were different from other families. They spoke openly about their internal struggle over the need to be "overprotective" when she was a child. They also shared their struggles over Carletta's independence. When our session ended, everyone in the Brown family described a sense of relief from being open and honest about their struggles. This family's strengths, especially related to their ability to communicate, as well as their loyalty and love for each other, impressed me.

After four individual sessions and three family sessions, everyone seemed more relaxed. The family reported feeling closer than ever. Mr. and Mrs. Brown said they understood Carletta's need to fit in at school, along with her need for independence. Carletta thanked her parents for their support in the past and for understanding her need to grow up. She also expressed that she understood how difficult it was for her parents to let her grow up.

For everyone involved, the challenge in therapy revolved around addressing Carletta's anger. Because of the personal, cultural, and religious factors described earlier, everyone in the family was cut-off from recognizing anger. As I saw it at the time, resolving this critical issue could unlock the case. My initial strategy was to continue highlighting Carletta's growth. We talked about her ability to acknowledge and address her conflicting feelings and tasks (Rogers, 1961) regarding dependence versus independence, love, frustration, and her disease. Likewise, she owned her personal developmental and emotional processes and experienced her feelings with me, in the moment (Rogers, 1961).

During individual sessions, Carletta gradually began recognizing "fleeting" moments of anger in daily life. We were making progress. At first, she talked about remarks made by teachers or other students that angered her "a bit." We began exploring how she handled these moments of anger, both internally and externally. Quickly, she began identifying her internal self-talk (Ellis, 1993) about this emotion. A key moment in therapy occurred when Carletta heard herself say, "Good girls don't yell," a message made loud and clear by her faith and family.

The Turning Point

After three sessions, Carletta reflected on the work she had completed. She began recognizing and accepting the irrational and "shaming" voice that suppressed her anger at having been ill her whole life. She visibly struggled over whether it was safe to share this with me. Despite my assurances, she could not vocalize this experience. As a compromise, Carletta agreed to begin writing a journal about her feelings. In subsequent sessions, Carletta began sharing her journal. At first, she talked about her fear of being angry. In her family, anger unresolved by God meant that she was "bad."

Soon, Carletta began directly talking about her anger. At first, she expressed anger at "the treatment" for her diabetes. She recalled the shots, medicine, diet, regulated play, and exercise she suffered as a child. Almost immediately, Carletta vented her anger at the various doctors and nurses that were insensitive toward her. She identified anger at her "normal" friends and cousins who did not have to deal with such matters. As it turns out, Carletta was angry with most everyone who did not have to deal with her disease. Their normality made her angry. Why couldn't she be normal too?

Her most difficult hurdle to cross was to express her anger through the question, "why me?" For Carletta, the intersection of family and religious upbringing made this question precarious. In her family, "why me?" meant anger at God. According to Faiver, O'Brien, & Ingersoll (2000), because of the historic separation between psychology and religion, counselors and social workers must voice their willingness to discuss religious issues with clients, which I did. Carletta identified her parents and the church as the source of the statement, "good girls don't yell." She also explored the relative value of such a rule. Over time, she learned to accept her anger as a healthy and normal response to her condition.

The Family's Breakthrough

Ultimately, to address the larger question of, "why me?" and her anger at God, we needed to meet again as a family. In the next two family sessions, Carletta shared her progress and discussed the connection between her anger and sticking others with pins in school. Both parents supported her insight and expression.

However, the biggest hurdle was yet to come. Carletta had reached the moment when she needed to explore her anger at God in her father's presence. I took the lead. I brought up the topic of religion with her parents, paving the way for her by discussing the strengths that faith provided their family and their church community. I also talked about Carletta's growing understanding of God as a support to her regarding health problems, emotional problems, and spiritual problems.

Her father responded tentatively. First, he began talking about the need for God in all matters, health or others. I did not challenge him. Instead, I listened, quietly reminding him of the benefits Carletta had received from doctors, nurses, and her therapist. He said that he understood these as examples of health and emotion separate from spirituality. He settled back, returning to his outward support for Carletta.

This interaction was helpful. It displayed Mr. Brown's tendency to become a "preacher," when Carletta needed an accepting father. At that point, Carletta began a mostly cognitive discussion of her anger. At the end of her discussion, Carletta told her parents that she had begun to ask, "why me?" This was an important moment, and I braced for her father's response.

After a moment of silence, Mrs. Brown began tearfully describing her own pain and anger at watching her eldest child undergo such intrusive and repeated medical procedures. She clearly and freely talked about her own rage and helplessness at not being able to protect her little girl from the never-ending needles.

I noticed Mr. Brown crying. After his wife finished, he began describing his prayers and faith in God as his way through the pain. He became the preacher again, using the same tone, I'm sure, as he used with parishioners. Sadly, his comments and tone squelched the emotional discussion for everyone in the family, including him.

I saw this as Carletta's decisive moment. I needed to address the family dynamics in this session. I quietly asked the family to reflect on what happens when father begins speaking as a pastor. Both mom and Carletta began by praising him for reminding them of the ways God could help. I pushed them further toward talking about what else happened, specifically asking about their tears and emotions during those times.

After a long and agonizing silence, Mr. Brown suddenly began talking about his own feelings of helplessness to protect his daughter. He spoke about his desire to be strong for his wife and daughter. He stated that he now understood how his process had cut him off from being available to his family when they hurt. This was the turning point for Carletta. Her father essentially gave her permission to experience her anger differently. He also allowed Carletta to see him differently too.

When Mr. Brown realized that his religious tone squelched their ability to experience and express emotion, we began discussing how gender roles and his profession affected Mr. Brown as well. Just as traditional gender roles had stifled Carletta's autonomy and ability to recognize and express anger, the same traditions stopped Mr. Brown from experiencing his own vulnerability in the face of his daughter's pain. He had learned early that his role as father, male, and preacher required "strength and leadership." In his effort to be a strong leader, he lost contact with his emotions, failing to realize the cost to his family and himself of cutting himself off from his own feelings.

At this point, Carletta's brother spoke about his concern for Carletta, and his confusion over his own feelings. The entire family began recognizing the importance of being open with each other, specifically related to emotional expression. I worked to solidify their gains, highlighting their strengths in exploring their hidden feelings together. Once the change began, it came suddenly.

Health Risks

While you may empathize with Carletta, the importance of understanding Carletta's emotions and anger in relation to her diabetes management is important. According to Jack (2003), "Health care providers should ask parents to be mindful of anger expressed through physical aggression and destruction of property" (p. 164). As adolescents transition into adulthood, they struggle with feelings of ambivalence and may intentionally engage in health-compromising behaviors (Weissberg-Benchell et al., 1995). The risks are well documented in the literature (Brage, 1995; Beeney, Bakry, & Dunn, 1996). Because of her diabetes, this was especially risky behavior for Carletta.

While the risks of health-compromising behaviors in diabetic adolescents are obvious, what may be less obvious is the longer-term mental health risk for diabetic adolescents. Jacobsen and colleagues (1997) found that while there were no differences in psychological disorders between adolescents with diabetes and other chronic illness, diabetic adolescents did report lower confidence and self-esteem. Biologically, diabetic adolescent girls are prone to involuntary weight gain during puberty, a time of heightened consciousness regarding body image. Some believe that insulin treatment is responsible for the weight gain (Jack, 2003).

Moreover, the importance of family therapy with chronic disease is also well documented (Mengal, Lawler, & Volk, 1992; Delameter et al., 1991). Generally, theorists believe that parents unable to provide emotional support and medical monitoring place their children at elevated risk for stress and subsequent health-compromising behaviors (Patterson, 1991).

Gender and Religion as Issues in Therapy

While Carletta and her family illustrated the importance of careful and deliberate engagement, a focus on strengths (Saleebey, 1997), and the importance of tentative interpretation, the more important lessons may lie in the careful assessment and judicial exploration of the affects of gender and religion in this case. While I never didactically taught Carletta or her parents about these issues or used "bibliotherapy" so they could read about divergent views on the topic, the issue was central in our work together. Carletta's unique interpretation of her parents' unspoken teachings about gender, faith, and emotions left Carletta alone and confused with her feelings, despite their constant love and concern.

As a social work educator, I believe that social workers must approach clients from different religious or cultural backgrounds carefully, reflecting on their own beliefs as a way to manage responses that could be offensive to clients. In this case, I was working with a daughter from a traditional patriarchal family with conservative religious beliefs. When this occurs, it is important that our own feminist-trained responses and/or religious beliefs do not become part of the therapy.

Often, social work educators do not prepare students to work with these issues. We disadvantage students because we often teach from a position and in a context that is hostile to exploring religious beliefs, either the students' or their clients'. This often stems from the tendency in academia to laud all things cognitive. Ignoring these issues also allows us to avoid the problems caused by tenets of some religious teachings that might contradict the NASW Code of Ethics (www.social-workers.org). For example, some faiths require believers to be evangelical, or crusade for converts. How does the social worker raised in these traditions manage the Code of Ethic's requirement for client self-determination?

For example, if my upbringing said that people from non-Christian religions are sinners that need saving and I am personally charged with converting others, how do I respect a client's right to self-determination if he or she is non-Christian? Moreover, where can students and practitioners find a venue to discuss these issues in an open and honest manner?

Likewise, another pitfall for a newly enthused feminist social work student would have occurred in this case if they had directly challenged, or even attempted to teach Carletta or her family about the negative impact of patriarchy. As someone born and raised in the same geographic and cultural environment as Carletta, I easily recognized her role. I knew from firsthand experience the cultural emphasis on being a "good girl," the rules about good girls being polite, quiet, nonathletic, compliant, nonsexual, and so on. Unless alternatives arise to challenge these beliefs, people never know that their cultural environment plays a role in their lives. Higher education provides, among other things, a feminist education as a basis for reevaluating one's identity and an opportunity for critical self-reflection. Thankfully, social work education provides these opportunities.

How then does the student or social worker in a situation like the one described above avoid the pitfall of teaching or preaching about their new insights? It is important to remember that practitioners have an obligation to understand clients, not make clients understand them. The basics of practice education includes the notion that practitioners must learn to separate their beliefs from client beliefs, and that simply because a practitioner observes something, does not mean they must point it out or comment on their observations. The ability to contain one's personal beliefs and values is an important practice skill (Schulman, 1998). Judicious utilization of insight or hunches can be a building block to success. Recognizing the way to weave or offer insights back to the client requires skill and practice that begins with the initial use of containment.

Termination

Carletta and her family terminated after three months in therapy. At the time of termination, Carletta was no longer acting out, and the family was communicating differently that before. A few months later, I contacted the family to follow-up on their progress. Carletta and her parents reported that she was no longer having problems at school. The family also stated their willingness to seek treatment in the future if problems arose. Surprisingly, they also agreed to speak with their physician about the role of stress in diabetes management.

  This case was successful because we included the family and were able to find the appropriate venue for them to discover new ways to relate to each other. By using the advanced generalist approach to explore various multi-systemic issues such as culture and religion, we were able to forge the type of professional relationship that allowed the Browns to deal directly with their feelings, without compromising their fundamental belief systems.

Questions

The author presented an interesting, successfully terminated case. Taking a broad view of this case, reevaluate the author's work and your participation through the questions asked throughout the case.

  1. Take a moment to review Carletta's progress in treatment. Based on the author's description, the professional literature, and the latest practice evidence, what occurred to account for her progress?

  2. What was the theoretical approach or combination of approaches that appeared to work best for Carletta and her family?

  3. Based on the work you have done earlier, what additional intervention(s) would you recommend for Carletta? Use the literature and latest evidence to justify your recommendations.

  4. Overall, what is your professional opinion of the work performed in this case? As always, refer to the professional literature, practice evidence, your experience, and the experience of student-colleagues when developing your opinion.

  5. Based on this review, what additional or alternative approaches could have been used with this case? That is, if you were the practitioner, how would you have approached this case? Please explain and justify your approach.

  6. What did this case demonstrate that you could use in other practice settings. List the most important things you learned by studying this case and how you could use them in your practice career.

Bibliography

Beeney, L. J., Bakry, A. A., Dunn, & S. M. (1996). Patient psychological and information needs when the diagnosis is diabetes. *Patient Education and Counseling, 29:* 109–116.

Brage, D. G. (1995). Adolescent depression: A review of the literature. *Archives of Psychiatric Nursing, 9:* 45–55.

Carter, B., & McGoldrick, M. (1988). Overview: The changing family life cycle: A framework for family therapy. In B. Carter & M. McGoldrick (eds.), *The changing family life cycle* (2nd ed., pp. 3–28). New York: Gardner.

Corey, G. (1996). *Theory and practice of counseling and psychotherapy, fifth edition.* Brooks/Cole: Pacific Grove, CA.

Delameter, A. M., Smith, J. A., Bubb, J., Green-Davis, S., Gamble, T., White, N. H., & Santiago, J. V. (1991). Family-based behavior therapy for diabetic adolescents. In J. H. Johnson and S. B. Johnson (eds.), *Advances in child health psychology.* Gainesville, FL, University of Florida Press, 293–306.

Ellis, A. (1993). Fundamentals of rational-emotive therapy. In W. Dryden and L. K. Hill (eds.), *Innovations in rational-emotive therapy* (pp.1–32). Newbury Park, CA: Sage.

Faiver, C. M., O'Brien, E. M., & Ingersoll, R. E. (2000). Religion, guilt, & mental health. *Journal of Counseling and Development 78:* 2, 155–162.

Jack, L., Jr. (2003). Biopsychosocial factors affecting metabolic control among female adolescents with type 1 diabetes. *Diabetes Spectrum, 16.* (Summer 2003): 164.

Jacobsen, A. M., Hauser, S. T., Willett, J. B., Wolfsdorf, J. I., Dvorak, R., Herman, E., & deGroot, M. (1997). Psychological adjustment to IDDM: 10-year follow-up of an onset cohort of child and adolescent patients. *Diabetes Care 20:* 811–818.

Juvenile Diabetes Research Foundation. [Online]. Available at http://www.jdrf.org/index.cfm.

Kelly, J. A. & Hansen, D. J. (1987). Social interactions and adjustment. In V. B. Van Hasselt and M. Hersen (eds.), *Handbook of adolescent psychology.* Pergamon Press: New York.

Haley, J. (1980). *Leaving home: The therapy of disturbed young people.* New York: McGraw-Hill.

Haley, J. (1976). *Problem-solving therapy.* New York: Harper Colophon Books.

Hunter Women's College Collective (1995). *Women's realities women's choices* (2nd ed.). Oxford University Press.

Lipman-Blumen, J. (1984). *Gender roles and power.* Englewood Cliffs, NJ: Prentice-Hall.

Mengal, M. B., Lawler, M. K., & Volk, R. J. (1992). Parental stress response within a family context: Association with diabetic control in adolescents with IDDM. *Family Systems Medicine 10:* 395–404.

Murphy, B. C., & Dillon, C. (2003). *Interviewing in action: Relationship, process, and change, second edition.* Pacific Grove, CA: Brooks/Cole.

National Association of Social Workers (1996). Code of Ethics, www.socialworkers.org.

Patterson, J. (1991). Chronic illness in children and the impact on families. In C. Childman, E. Nunnally, and F. Cox (eds.), *Chronic illness and disability.* Beverly Hills, CA: Sage, 1988, 69–107.

Rogers, C. (1961). *On becoming a person: A therapist's view of psychotherapy.* Boston, MA: Houghton Mifflin.

Saleebey, D. (1997). *The strengths perspective in social work practice, second edition.* New York: Longman.

Schulman, L. (1998). *Interactional supervision* (4th ed.) Washington, DC: NASW Press.

Siepker, B., & Kandaras, C. (1985). *Group therapy with children and adolescents: A treatment manual.* New York: Human Sciences Press.

Weissberg-Benchell, J., Glasgow, A. M., Tynan, W. D., Wirtz, P., Turek, J., & Ward, J. (1995). Adolescent diabetes management and mismanagement. *Diabetes Care 18:* 77–82.